GRAPHIC

DESIGN

20TH

CENTURY

1890-1990

Princeton Architectural Press
37 East Seventh Street
New York, New York 10003

For a free catalog of books, call
1.800.722.6657.
Visit our web site at www.papress.com.

Published simultaneously in The
Netherlands by V+K Publishing/Design,
Laren

For Princeton Architectural Press:
Project editor: Nicola Bednarek
Special thanks to: Nettie Aljian, Janet
Behning, Megan Carey, Penny (Yuen Pik)
Chu, Russell Fernandez, Jan Haux, Clare
Jacobson, Mark Lamster, Nancy Eklund
Later, Linda Lee, Katharine Myers, Jane
Sheinman, Scott Tennent, Jennifer
Thompson, Joseph Weston, and Deb Wood
of Princeton Architectural Press –Kevin C.
Lippert, publisher

Library of Congress Cataloging-in-
Publication Data [TK]

ISBN 1-56898-414-6
Printed in Belgium

Princeton Architectural Press
New York

GRAPHIC

DESIGN

20TH

CENTURY

Alston W. Purvis

Martijn F. Le Coultre

GRAPHIC

DESIGN

20TH

CENTURY

1890-1990

Contents

Preface

Graphic design is all around us. Although we live in a time of mass communication by means of radio, TV, and Internet, graphic design is still the driving force behind most effective forms of communication. Images can be gripping, they can haunt you in your sleep. Slogans are mere shouts in the distance. A readable Internet page is as much graphic design as a poster printed in the 1890s or a newspaper advertisement from even earlier times.

Selling a product, an idea or simply conveying a message is therefore best done by visual means. Illustrations tell a story, and the earliest scripts are not without reason based on symbols - from hieroglyphs to characters. In the end, type itself became a form of graphic design.

While selecting images for a book on graphic design one wonders what happened to all the posters and enamel signs that one can see in photos of street scenes of a bygone era. Most of us, at some stage of our lives, have collected postage stamps and thus graphic design. We were taught to handle these precious small pieces of paper with the utmost care. We bought special albums to file them in a certain order. And we proudly showed the results to elderly aunts. Those aunts then in turn gave us stamps that they, or their long deceased husbands, had collected. While doing so they unconsciously set in motion a chain of preservation.

Unfortunately, most types of graphic design were not as collectible as stamps. Most advertisements, posters, and enamel signs were of a more ephemeral nature. Used, forgotten, and thrown away. Only their message lived on.

Today it is not easy to put together an overview of international graphic design. There exists no institution that systematically collects information on a global scale about designers and their production. As a private collector I know that in many museums around the world large troves can be found, but that most curators do not know what they actually have in storage. Nor do they know when and by whom certain pieces were designed or how they were produced.

Looking through this book one should realize that what is being shown here is only the tip of the iceberg and therefore must be incomplete. We owe this compilation to the collectors from earlier times. I sincerely hope it wets your appetite.

Martijn F. Le Coultre
Laren, The Netherlands

Alston W. Purvis

Graphic Design
20th Century

**Stenberg Brothers Georgi & Vladimir Augustovich
Stenberg** c. 1927, poster. 105.5 x 76 cm, USSR.
(French film: The Miracle of the Wolves.)

Alston W. Purvis

Graphic Design
20th Century

Although the term was rarely used until after World War II, the American book and type designer William Addison Dwiggins referred to his own work as "graphic design" as early as 1922. Compared to painting, sculpture and architecture, "graphic design" was a relatively new artistic field, and historians of the field like Philip B. Meggs helped to make it an historical discipline as well.

During the Industrial Revolution a dramatic growth in advertising necessitated changes in printing technology. The Linotype machine, patented in 1886 by Otto Mergenthaler in Baltimore, enabled printers to cast and recycle lines of lead text. One year later in England, Tolbert Lanston invented the Monotype machine that could cast individual letters. The first automated lithographic steam press was used in 1868 and the first offset press in 1906. Yet, although printing technology expanded, craftsmanship, design, and a concern for quality became secondary considerations, and by the 1870s a nadir was reached in European and American graphic design. However, as the century drew to a close, there were signs of new beginnings that would become bridges to the twentieth century. Responding to the

Mucha, Alfons Maria (litho F. Champenois, Paris, 1896.) 205 x 71 cm, France

impersonal and visually barren nature of machine-made products, William Morris began the Kelmscott Press in 1890. Morris advocated a design renewal through returning to the craftsmanship of the Middle Ages, and with the Arts and Crafts movement began a crusade to restore lost principles in type design and printing.

Art Nouveau was the most important European modern art movement at the turn of the century. In addition to forms derived from nature, sources included medieval manuscripts and decorative arts from India, Syria, Egypt, Persia, Japan, and the Dutch East Indies. The movement used elegant undulating lines and flat planes filled with detail, and was often accompanied by an arcane symbolism. Extensively used in architecture, fabric design, and the industrial arts, it was especially manifest in graphic design.

Art Nouveau inspired many artists to break with academic art and unite into autonomous groups. The Vienna Secession began on April 3, 1897, when some of the younger and more progressive members of the Künstlerhaus, the Vienna creative artists group, walked out in protest against the association's conservatism. A square format was used for *Ver Sacrum*, their monthly publication begun in 1898, which for six years displayed original etchings, lithographs, and woodcuts by Secessionist artists. It also included articles about individual artists, an illustrated monthly calendar, critical essays, reviews of exhibitions, and poems and other writing by contemporary authors. To insure harmony, advertisers could use only artists contributing to particular issues.

Peter Behrens and Henri van de Velde, both with Art Nouveau backgrounds, were leaders in the Deutsche Werkbund instituted in 1907. Although inspired by the Arts and Crafts movement, Behrens and Van de Velde stressed the involvement of artists in industry. Behrens produced the first corporate identity when he designed the architecture, advertising, products, logo, and printed work for the AEG (General Electric Company) in Germany.

14

Richter, Hans 1919, poster. 140 x 96 cm, Germany

Lucian Bernhard's 1906 design for Priester matches produced a radical change in advertising posters. The result of a design contest, it depicted two matchsticks and the word *Priester* on a plain background. This generated the "plakatstil" (poster style) emphasizing clarity and simplicity. In addition to Bernhard, designers working in this mode included Hans Rudi Erdt and Julius Klinger, an Austrian who began in the Vienna Secession. The most urbane adherent to the plakatstil style was the Munich designer Ludwig Hohlwein, who initiated a cosmopolitan style that would significantly influence advertising poster design in the twentieth century. With simple lettering framed by rectangles, large flat areas of color, and an economy of means, his approach recalls that of the Beggarstaffs a decade earlier in England. Also influenced by the plakatstil was the American Edward McKnight Kauffer, who moved to London in 1914, where he designed 131 posters for the London Underground. In a 1918 poster for the *Daily Herald* he successfully utilized cubist and futurist elements in commercial design. With his 1908 poster for the resort town of Zermatt, Emil Cardinaux designed the first Swiss poster similar to the German plakatstil, and, inspired by Cardinaux, a clear trend was evident in Swiss posters by 1910. With realistic images and simple typography this became known as Basel realism. Leading designers were Niklaus Stoecklin and Otto Baumberger, whose posters were characterized by a hyperrealistic approach.

Graphic design was an essential propaganda tool during World War I. Some of the British and American posters appealed to sentimentality. Others were more straightforward such as James Montgomery Flagg's 1917 recruiting poster depicting Uncle Sam pointing an accusing finger at potential recruits. The German designers Bernhard, Gipkins, Erdt, and Hohlwein all produced posters eloquently supporting the Axis war effort.

The invention of Linotype and Monotype generated a resurgence of typeface design. Morris F. Benton, director of type design at the American Type Founders Company

Marinetti, Filippo Achille Emilio (Filippo Tommaso)
1932 cover from his futurist book 'Parole in Liberta'
printed on metal

Schwitters, Kurt Cover of Merz 1, Hannover 1923

(ATF), was influential in reviving past designs. His own typefaces include Alternate Gothic, Century Schoolbook, Cloister Bold, Franklin Gothic, News Gothic, Souvenir, and Stymie Medium. Letters on Trajan's column inspired Perpetua, the first typeface by the English designer Eric Gill. His popular sans-serif typeface Gill Sans was inspired by the Railway type designed by his former teacher Edward Johnston in 1916. Dwiggins' eighteen typefaces for Linotype include Electra in 1935 and Caledonia in 1938, the latter becoming one of the most popular book types of the twentieth century.

Fervently embracing the modern age, the Italian futurists discarded old notions of harmony as they expressed speed and movement in visual design. Using type cut from newspapers and magazines, they produced poems reflecting the noise of the modern world. Futurism began when the Italian poet Filippo Marinetti published his *Manifesto of Futurism* on February 20, 1909:

> We affirm that a new beauty has enriched the world's magnifi-
> cence: the beauty of speeds .... Except in struggle, there is no
> more beauty. No work without an aggressive character can be a
> masterpiece.... We will destroy museums, libraries, and fight
> against moralism, feminism, and all utilitarian cowardice.

Sharing some of the objectives of Futurism, Dada began as a literary movement when the poet Hugo Ball started the Cabaret Voltaire in Zurich as a meeting place for young poets. Chance placement and absurd titles characterized their graphic work. Its leader, the young and volatile Paris-based Romanian poet Tristan Tzara, presented the Dada message as if firing it from a pistol:

> I am against systems, the most acceptable system is on principle
> to have none.... Dada; a protest with the fists of its whole being
> engaged in destructive action: Dada; knowledge of all the means
> rejected up until now by the shamefaced sex of comfortable
> compromise and good manners: Dada; abolition of logic, which is
> the dance of the impotent to create.

18

Klutsis, Gustav Gustavovic 'The USSR is the Avant
Garde of the World Proletariat.' Poster. 144 x 104 cm, USSR

Dada quickly spread to other parts of Europe. Although the dadaists contended they were not making art, they still made lasting contributions to graphic design. These include a further exploration of expressive typography and the invention of photomontage, a design process where, though using radical contrasts, parts of photographs are combined into new images. Turned down for membership in Dada for being too "bourgeois," the Hannover artist Kurt Schwitters started his own brand of Dada called Merz. Beginning in 1919, he made collages from printed ephemera and found materials, combining Dada elements of nonsense and chance with a strong design sensibility.

John Heartfield, the English name used by Helmut Herzfeld to protest German militarism, became a founder of the Berlin Dada faction in 1919. Through posters, magazine covers, and illustrations, Heartfield used photomontage as a propaganda weapon against the Weimar Republic and the Nazi party. Cutting photographs from magazines and newspapers, his direct images were easily understood by the working class.

The Russian constructivists rejected the idea of unique art works and aimed to erase the separation of art and labor. They aggressively sought a utilitarian design related to industry and propaganda and new art forms to serve the proletariat. For them, photography and offset printing were ideal methods to promote communism. El Lissitzky, one of the leading Russian constructivists, created his more enduring work in book and poster design and was one of the first to fully exploit photomontage as a communication medium. His book designs combined abstraction and functionalism with illustrations made from type shop material. Lissitzky had considerable influence outside of Russia, launching magazines in Berlin and Switzerland. Alexander Rodchenko, also an early user of photomontage, applied it with penetrating effec-tiveness. The master of Russian political photomontage was Gustav Klutsis, referring to it as the "art of socialism's construction." After Russian film companies were nationalized in 1923, Georgi and Vladimir Stenberg took the lead in film poster design.

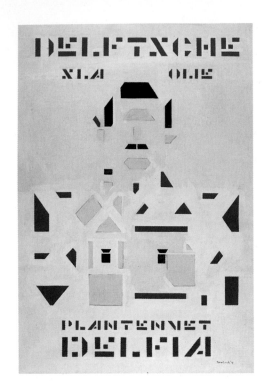

van der Leck, Bart Anthony 1919, gouache. Final version of twelve designs for a poster for the Delft Salad Oil Factories. 89 x 59.5 cm, The Netherlands

In The Netherlands, De Stijl, one of many iconoclastic responses to the tragedy of World War I, was established in 1917 by Theo Van Doesburg and others including the architect J.J.P. Oud and the painters Vilmos Huszár and Piet Mondrian. The architect Jan Wils, the furniture designer and architect Gerrit Rietveld, the painters and designers Bart van der Leck and Cesar Domela Nieuwenhuis, and the film producer Hans Richter soon joined them. Similar to Constructivism, an objective was to cleanse art of subject matter, illusion, ornamentation, and subjectivity. De Stijl's first manifesto was published in 1918:

> There is an old and a new awareness of time. The old is based on the individual. The new is based on the universal. The struggle of the individual against the universal is manifesting itself in the World War as well as in contemporary art.

Volume 1, Number I of their official journal *De Stijl* appeared in October 1917. Huszár designed the covers of the first three volumes, and, after being redesigned by Van Doesburg and Mondrian at the end of 1920, *De Stijl* reflected the influence of El Lissitsky and Schwitters. Like Constructivism and Futurism, De Stijl endorsed industrial culture and was the most significant Dutch contribution to architecture and design in the twentieth century.

The Dutch designer Hendrik Nicolaas Werkman fits into no convenient drawer of modern graphic design history. Characteristics of his work are playfulness, experimentation, and an unwavering optimism. Since he was using the basic letterpress, subtleties such as the oddities of wood grains, scratches on used pieces of type, disparate methods of inking, and paper textures all play a role in his work.

In 1918 the Dutch architect Hendricus Theodorus Wijdeveld introduced the magazine *Wendingen*, at first devoted to architecture, construction, and ornamentation, but which would for thirteen years represent all sectors of the visual arts. In its design,

Schlemmer, Oskar 1918, poster. 65 x 51 cm, Germany.

Wijdeveld used solid and heavy borders constructed from right angles, a typographic reflection of the brick architecture of the Amsterdam School.

The Bauhaus opened in Weimar in 1919 with Walter Gropius becoming its first director and originator of its name. Goals included a unity of art and craft and utile designs with functional forms. The Bauhaus helped to engender a revolution in typography, and many artists associated with it significantly affected the graphic design field. The Hungarian Laszlo Moholy-Nagy expanded photography as a design tool. After studying at the Bauhaus, Herbert Bayer was made the master of the typographic workshop and created the Universal typeface that was a basis for Paul Renner's Futura in 1927. In 1925 the Bauhaus moved to Dessau, and after seven years it was closed due to Nazi pressure. A brief attempt to revive it in Berlin ended in 1933.

Jan Tschichold eloquently presented his ideas about a new functional typography in his 1928 book, *Die Neue Typographie:*

> The essence of the New Typography is clarity. This places it in deliberate opposition to the old typography whose aim was "beauty" and whose clarity did not attain the high level we require today. The utmost clarity is necessary today because of the manifold claims for our attention made by the extraordinary amount of print, which demands the greatest economy of expression.

After being arrested by the Nazis, Tschichold and his wife fled to Basel in 1933 where in 1938 he produced his last designs using principles of asymmetric typography. Tschichold formally forswore asymmetrical typography and the sans-serif in 1946, writing that *Die Neue Typographie's* "impatient attitude conforms to the German bent for the absolute." Ironically, Tschichold would design the magnificent sans-serif face Sabon in 1967.

Cassandre, A.M. (pseudonym for Adolphe Jean-Marie
Mouron), 1924, poster, Hachard & Cie, Paris. 217 x 132 cm,
France

Piet Zwart and Paul Schuitema were the leading Dutch constructivists. Trained as an architect, Zwart began working in graphic design at the age of thirty-six. Although influenced by De Stijl, he rejected its reliance on horizontals and verticals, and his dynamic layouts often employed diagonals. Zwart referred to himself as a typotekt, a combination of the words typographer and architect.

In 1937 Zwart defined the designer's role:

> It is the task of functional typography to establish the typographical look of our time, free, in so far as it is possible, from tradition; to activate typographic forms; to define the shape of new typographic problems, methods, and techniques, and discard the guild mentality.

Schuitema's inventive use of photomontage raised everyday assignments to dynamic heights. In 1961 he reflected on the innovative years of the 1920s and 1930s:

> Every thing, every letter, every picture, every sound, every color should have its function.... A letter was to serve the function of reading, nothing else. It had to have distinct, objective and clear forms, it was not supposed to be elegant, beautiful, or feminine. Its beauty is its function, there should be nothing else mysterious behind or beside it.

Art Deco was the popular international style during the 1930s. Although it can be seen as a last extension of Art Nouveau, its geometric-based forms reflect Cubism, Futurism and Dada, as well as historical connections such as Greece and Egypt. In Paris, the Art Deco designer A.M. Cassandre assimilated concepts of contemporary artists, Fernand Léger and Le Corbusier in particular, and applied them to his poster designs. Beginning in 1923, he would dominate French advertising art for sixteen years. As an indication of his respect for lettering he designed Bifur in 1929, the most popular Art Deco display face, and Peignot in 1937.

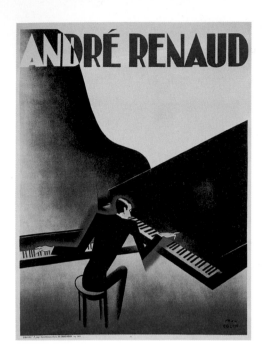

Colin, Paul André Renaud 1929, poster. Succes, H. Chachoin, Paris. 159 x 113 cm, France

The Hungarian designer and theoretician Gyorgy Kepes described Cassandre's method in *Language of Vision* published in 1944.

> One unifying device employed by Cassandre was the use of a contour line common to various spatial units. The double outline takes on a double meaning, similar to a visual pun. It refers to inside and outside space simultaneously, and the spectator is therefore forced into intensive participation as he seeks to resolve the apparent contradiction. But the equivocal contour line does more than unify different spatial data. It acts like a warp, weaving the threads of color planes into one rhythmical unity. The rhythmical flow of the line injects the picture surface with a sensual intensity.

Among the first to grasp the significance of new reproduction techniques was Herbert Matter, who had worked in Paris with Léger and Cassandre. Between 1934 and 1936, he designed monumental travel posters for the Swiss National Tourist Office combining both photomontage and illustration.

Paul Colin's earliest designs date from 1925 when he was asked to design graphics and sets for the Théâtre des Champs-Elysées in Paris. Always maintaining an uncomplicated approach to his work, he became the most prolific French graphic designer of his generation.

Leading designers in Czechoslovakia were Ladislav Sutnar and the radical constructivist Karel Teige, both using photomontage in an incisive manner. Sutnar supported the constructivist objective to have design standards apply to all aspects of modern life and designed furniture, silverware, dishes, fabrics, and toys in addition to his prodigious output in graphic design.

Bringing with them the objective ideas of Modernism and the conceptual symbolism

28

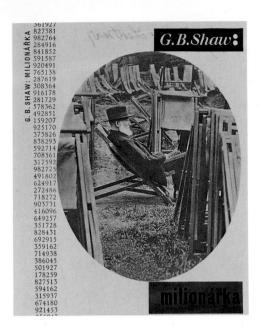

Sutnar, Ladislav 1934 wrapper for Millionarka by G.B. Shaw

of Surrealism, many designers immigrated to the United States in the 1930s because of the political situations in Europe and Russia. Alexey Brodovitch came from the Soviet Union in 1930 and after becoming art director of *Harper's Bazaar* in 1934 exerted an unprecedented influence on magazine design. Those leaving Germany included Bayer, who was made art director for the Container Corporation of America; Will Burtin, who became art director at *Fortune Magazine* and Marcel Breuer and Gropius, who both taught architecture at Harvard. Joseph Binder was widely popular after arriving from Austria in 1934. Matter left Switzerland and produced noteworthy designs and photography for the Container Corporation of America, *Vogue, Fortune, Harper's Bazaar,* and Knoll Associates. Also Swiss, Erik Nitsche became art director for Saks Fifth Avenue. Sutner happened to be in the United States when Germany annexed Czechoslovakia in 1939, and in addition to setting up a studio in New York he taught at Pratt Institute. Hungary contributed Moholy-Nagy, who established the short-lived New Bauhaus in Chicago and Gyorgy Kepes, who taught visual design at the Massachusetts Institute of Technology. Similar to Sutner, the French designer Jean Carlu was stranded in New York while working on a French exhibition for the New York World's Fair when France surrendered in 1940. There were others as well, and American graphic design was forever enriched by their presence.

During World War II, graphic design was a vital propaganda medium, and painters, illustrators, and designers, many of them immigrants, received commissions from the U.S. Office of War Information (OWI). These included Binder, McKnight Kauffer, Bayer, and Matter. Carlu's "Construction" poster was such a success that he was hired as an advisor by the OWI.

The International Style was the most important Swiss contribution to graphic design following World War II. Reliable and predictable, it was based on logical analysis and an objective presentation of information. As designers, educators, and theoreticians, Josef Müller-Brockmann and Armin Hofmann played dominant roles in its development. Others connected with the International Style included Max Bill and Anton

Matter, Herbert 1934, poster. 102 x 64 cm, Switzerland

Stankowski. Bill returned to Zurich in 1929 after studying for two years at the Bauhaus. Although his major work consisted of posters, his corporate identities, book covers, and advertising are monumental in scope. The German-born painter and graphic designer Stankowski worked from 1929 until 1937 in Zurich where he came into contact with many leading Swiss designers including Bill and Matter. His work was reinforced through his understanding of science and research.

In 1947 Armin Hofmann began teaching at the Basel School of Design where he developed a design system founded on basic elements and a dynamic formal unity. Müller-Brockmann sought a universal, impersonal, clear, and objective graphic language. In his book, *The Graphic Designer and His Design Problems*, he outlined his design mission in precise terms:

> The Designer must know and accept the technical possibilities
> of modern typography and, instead of striving for ornamental
> effects, he must be able to see his plan as a formal conception.
> This economic, timesaving, and practical method of composition
> is consonant with our age of technical perfection and clarity.

In 1954 Adrian Frutiger, a Swiss designer living in Paris, completed his design of the Univers font family. In the mid-1950s, together with Max Miedinger, Edouard Hoffman of the HAAS type foundry in Switzerland designed the Neue Haas Grotesk, which the Frankfurt foundry D. Stempel AG would produce as Helvetica in 1961. A native of Nuremberg, Herman Zapf designed more than fifty typefaces for the Stempel foundry. His background as a calligrapher and his profound knowledge of type history strengthened his sensitivity to letterforms.

Willem Sandberg, director of the Stedelijk Museum in Amsterdam from 1945 to 1962, was an influential Dutch designer during the postwar period. In posters and catalogues he often used letters made from torn paper, a technique later taken up by Yusaku Kamekura in Japan. Like Dick Elffers, Sandberg avoided being associated

32

Lenica, Jan 1956, poster. Rio Escondido. 86.5 x 59 cm,
Poland

with particular movements. Although Elffers had worked with Zwart and Schuitema during the 1930s, he never became a constructivist and often combined montage with line drawings. After the war he changed to a more painterly style. The first design group in The Netherlands, Total Design, was founded by Wim Crouwel and four others in 1963. They not only designed publications but the total image as well, thus the origin of their name.

After World War II, Western influences were prominent among Japanese designers. Many, such as Kamekura, applied European Constructivism while retaining Japanese traditions. More than any other designer, Kamekura influenced the development of graphic design in Japan and helped to create a working understanding between designers and industry. In another realm, Tadanori Yokoo, a cult figure for the postwar generation, used comic book art, engravings, photographs, Japanese prints, pop art, and psychedelic themes as sources.

Polish designers developed a strong national style during the 1950s and 1960s. Their designs, especially posters, incorporated painted illustrations, photography, and hand lettering and were infused with symbolism, metaphors, and a unique adaptation of surrealism. Among the most notable designers were Henryk Tomaszewski, Jan Lenica, Waldemar Swierzy, and Roman Cieslewicz. Unlike those in the Soviet Union, postwar poster designers in Poland were supported by government agencies, and clients included the theater, circus, opera, cinema, symphony orchestra, and tourism. Sadly, the removal of the iron curtain had a detrimental effect upon Polish design as government support evaporated and the influence of commercialism from Western Europe and the United States diluted its intensity.

In postwar Italy, Armando Testa and Giovanni Pintori were among the leading designers. Joining Olivetti as a designer in 1936, Pintori was art director from 1950 to 1968 and often resorted to a cryptic, poetic style where the only reference to the client was its name. In France, painted posters remained in vogue, and prewar artists

Rand, Paul 1950, poster. 104.5 x 68 cm, USA

like Colin were still active. Although having worked as an assistant to Cassandre, Raymond Savignac rejected Art Deco for a more whimsical approach with a "single image for a single idea."

In the United States, the older postwar poster generation included giants such as Paul Rand, Lester Beall, and Saul Bass. Noted for his work as a designer, educator, and writer on design, Rand remained a dominant and inspiring force until his death in 1996. At the age of twenty-three, he became art director of both *Esquire* and *Apparel Arts.* Four years later in 1941, he began working as art director for the William H. Weintraub Advertising Agency in New York where he helped to change the face of advertising in America. Rand set up an independent design firm in 1954 and was responsible for the corporate identities of major companies including IBM, Westinghouse, ABC, and UPS. Rand stressed that trademarks should be timeless, reduced to basic universal forms, visually unique, and functional, and his logos fulfill all of these criteria.

A native New Yorker, Saul Bass moved to Los Angeles in 1946 where he reinvented the design of American film titles. Bradbury Thompson, a native of Kansas, arrived in New York City in 1938. His clients included the West Virginia Pulp and Paper Company for whom he designed the Westvaco Inspirations.

In 1959 the Cuban revolution generated a singular school of poster design. Since commercial advertising ended with the revolution, posters were used to announce cultural events, public gatherings, and accomplishments of the new government. Cuba's eclectic designers exploited any style and, because of economic necessity, any technique.

In the United States during the 1960s, designers such as Milton Glaser, a founding member of Push Pin Studio, and Peter Max were among the most popular. Their design approach, at times celebrating the anti-establishment subculture, was later

Moscoso, Victor 1967, poster. 56 x 35.5 cm, USA

broadly labeled by the media as "psychedelic." Wes Wilson, a true originator of this style, actually stated that his colors were often the result of experiments with LSD. The most influential of this genre in California was Victor Moscoso, who achieved vibrant optical effects through color and hand-drawn letters distorted almost to the point of illegibility. During the turbulent latter half of the sixties, protest groups, especially students, strongly reacted to events such as the war in Vietnam, and for them graphic design was an essential tool. In addition to lesser known designers, established figures such as Rand, Ivan Chermayeff, Glaser, and Seymour Chwast contributed anti-war posters.

Display type was still set in metal at the beginning of the 1960s but was soon replaced by phototypography. This gave the designer total control over letterspacing and type sizes, and letters could be extended, condensed, or italicized from a single film base. Herb Lubalin, immensely popular among young American designers, ingeniously employed phototypography as an expressive medium.

New German designers included Gunter Rambow, who explored theatrical effects with modern photographic techniques. His posters often use one image made from montage elements with the title playing a supportive role. In The Netherlands, many continued to enrich the graphic design field. Among others, these include Jan Bons, Nicolaas Wijnberg, Gerard Werners, Benno Wissing, Wim Crouwel, Pieter Brattinga, and Gert Dumbar and designers associated with his studio. Independent and diametrically opposed styles are the painterly and melodic posters of Gielijn Escher and the confrontational photography-based style of Anthon Beeke. A conscious stylistic variance and discard of tradition marks the work of two explosive studios that arrived on the scene in the early 1980s, Hard Werken in Rotterdam and Wild Plakken in Amsterdam.

Beginning in the 1970s, type design experienced a rebirth in The Netherlands largely due to the inspiration of Gerrit Noordzij. Through his teaching at the Royal Academy

FF Kosmik OT

Autofflippperr*

0123456789 0123456789

Plain & **Bold** ¶ ✈ 🌐

✱In OpenType Savvy Applications

Liveliness, Onomatopaea

38

MACOS+WIN, SCREEN+PRINT

OpenTypeFontFont

van Blokland, Erik Letterfont Kosmik, 1992

of Fine Arts at The Hague many of his students went on to achieve notable results in this field. Among them were Erik van Blokland, Just van Rossum, and Noordzij's son Peter Matthias.

Based in Cambridge, Massachusetts, Matthew Carter first learned the traditional punch cutting of metal type at Enschedé in The Netherlands. His typefaces span the full range of typographic technology from metal type to our digital era, where he has helped to maintain the integrity of type design. Among others, his designs include Bell Centennial, Galliard, Mantinia, and Sophia.

Designers in the 1960s and 1970s began to seek other alternatives to the modernist and international styles. Although trained in traditional typesetting, Wolfgang Weingart became the leading designer of New Wave typography. Weingart came from Germany to study at the Basel School in 1964, and after joining the faculty in 1968 he soon questioned the minimal approach of his colleague Hofmann. In the mid-1970s, he began experimenting with offset printing, film, and collage, and by using layers of images, type, and the printing process he produced a unique integration of type and image. After studying with Weingart in the early 1970s, April Greiman set up a studio in Los Angeles. Creating a new sense of space depth using overlapping forms, diagonals, and reverse perspective, she became the most influential New Wave designer in California.

Complexity and Contradiction in Architecture, published by the architect Robert Venturi in 1966, provided the seeds for the broadly based style that would later be called Postmodernism. Rejecting the modernist approach of Gropius, Venturi promoted architecture based on historic forms and American vernacular. Although the label Postmodernism was initially used for architecture in the 1970s, it was soon applied to graphic design. Ambiguous as it might have been, Postmodernism was a convenient term for much of the graphic design that disputed the International Style's doctrines of harmony, legibility, and the grid.

Suokko, Glenn A. and Emigre Graphics Magazine
Emigre, 1988, cover

As with romanticism versus classicism, intuition took precedence over the intellect.

Another significant contribution came from Rudy Vanderlans and his wife Zuzana Licko through the magazine *Emigre* started in San Francisco in 1982. Trained in the Dutch modernist tradition at the Royal Academy of Fine Arts at The Hague, Vanderlans later questioned all graphic design traditions while using *Emigre* as a means for exploring new computer design technology.

Punk, part of the drug and pop music culture, provided another option for designers weary of Modernism. New typesetting methods were used in *The Face,* a magazine started in 1980 with a Punk design heritage. Its art director, the widely imitated Neville Brody, used highly volatile pages filled with layers of meaning and eccentric display types with overtones of Art Deco. Although influenced by Dada and Russian Constructivism, Brody maintains a painterly and extremely personal approach to his work. The American designer David Carson, who began working in graphic design during the 1980s, tossed the grid to the wind as he sought the expressive core of individual themes. As he turned up the volume of the page, all ideology and rules were relegated to the past.

Far ahead of his time in the 1950s, the Canadian Marshall McLuhan wrote that typesetting as begun by Gutenberg would eventually be replaced by electronic technology. No doubt, he would be astounded by the accuracy of his prediction. By the 1980s, instantaneous communications and computer technology radically changed the graphic design landscape, giving designers almost total command of design and production procedures. McLuhan also contended that "the medium is the message", and this is certainly often the case with contemporary graphic design. His position that "societies have always been shaped more by the nature of the media by which men communicate than by the content of the communication" seems more relevant today than ever before.

42

Kisman, Max 1986. Poster for a music festival in Amsterdam's Paradiso, The Netherlands

Although we have entered another period of radical technological innovation, traditional means of expression and aesthetic standards must retain their relevance. Philip Meggs fittingly wrote in the foreword to *A History of Graphic Design* "that if we understand the past, we will be better able to continue a culture legacy of beautiful form and effective communication. If we ignore this legacy, we run the risk of becoming buried in a mindless morass of a commercialism whose mole-like vision ignores human values and needs as it burrows forward into darkness."

Martijn F. Le Coutre

GRAPHIC

DESIGN

Legacy of Beautiful
Form and Effective
Communication

20TH

CENTURY

de Toulouse Lautrec, Henri (France 1864-1901), 1892,
printed by Edw. Ancourt, Paris, 146 x 96 cm, France.
(As the banker Rothschild thought he saw himself in
the main character of the book, he tried to stop the cir-
culation of this poster. It is therefore the only poster by
Lautrec that, at least officially, could not be bought at
the print dealer Arnould of Paris.)

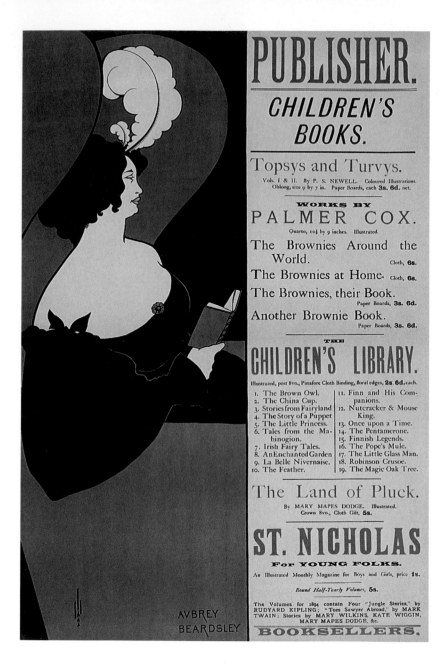

Beardsley, Aubrey Vincent (United Kingdom, Brighton 1872-France, Mentone 1898) 1894. 75.5 x 51 cm, United Kingdom

Toorop, Jan Theodoor (Java 1858-The Hague 1928) S. Lankhout & Co, The Hague, 1894. 100 x 70 cm, The Netherlands. (This poster for the Delft Salad Oil Factories was used for several years and made such a lasting impression that when the Dutch refer to 'Salad-Oil Style' they mean Art Nouveau.)

Bonnard, Pierre (France, Fontenay Aux Roses, Seine
1867-Le Cannet Near Cannes 1947) 1894, Imp. Edw.
Ancourt, Paris. 87.5 x 69 cm, France

Beggarstaff Brothers (James Pryde 1869-1941 &
William Nicholson 1872-1949), 1894, Henderson & Co,
Glasgow. 147 x 98 cm, United Kingdom

Steinlen, Theophile Alexandre (Switzerland,
Lausanne 1859-France, Paris 1923) 1896, Imp.
Charles Verneau, Paris. 140.5 x 100 cm, France

Art Nouveau was the most important European modern art movement at the turn of the century. In addition to forms derived from nature, sources included medieval manuscripts and decorative arts.

LA·DAME·AUX·CAMELIAS

SARAH BERNHARDT

THÉATRE DE LA RENAISSANCE

IMP. F. CHAMPENOIS. PARIS

Toorop, Jan Theodoor (Netherlands Indies,
Poerworedje, Java 1858-The Netherlands, The Hague
1928) 1896. Het Hooge Land. Beekbergen, S.Lankhout
& Co., Den Haag [od]. 95 x 68 cm, The Netherlands

Sütterlin, Ludwig (Germany) 1896. Berliner.
Otto von Holten, Berlin. G. Büxenstein & Cp. ph.
Berliner. 95 x 64 cm, Germany

Toorop, Jan Theodoor (Dutch Indies, Poerworedjo,
Java 1858-The Netherlands, The Hague 1928) 1898.
Arbeid voor de vrouw, S. Lankhout & Co, Den Haag.
The Netherlands

Thorn Prikker, Johan (The Netherlands, The Hague
1888-Germany, Cologne 1932) 1896, Lith. S. Lankhout,
The Hague, 135 x 100.5 cm, The Netherlands

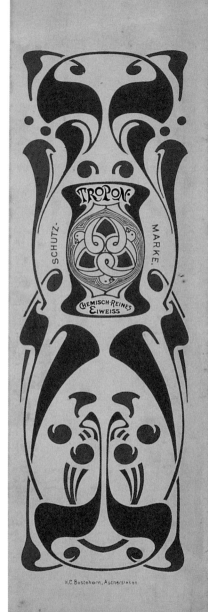

Velde, Henri Clemens van de (Belgium, Antwerp
1863-Switzerland, Zürich 1957) wrappers for a milk
carton, 67 x 43 cm, Germany, lithograph 1898

Klimt, Gustav (Austria, Vienna 1862-Vienna 1918)
1898, Lith. Anst. v. A. Berger, Vienna. 63.5 x 46 cm,
Austria

66

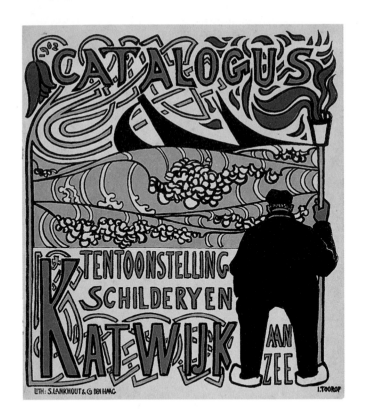

Toorop, Jan (Indonesia, Poerworedjo 1858-The
Netherlands, The Hague 1928) 1902 front cover for an
exhibition catalogue, lithography by S. Lankhout & Co,
The Hague

Cappiello, Leonetto (Italy, Livorno 1875- France, Nice 1942) 1901.
 Cachou Lajaunie. Imp. P. Vercasson & Cie, Paris. [od]. 134.5 x 94.5 cm, France

Olbrich, Joseph Maria (Silesia, Troppau 1867-
Germany, Düsseldorf 1908) 1901, Hofdruckerei H.
Hofman, Darmstadt. 86 x 50 cm, Germany

Forstner, Leopold (Leonfelden, Austria 1878-
Stockerau, Austria, 1936) coverdesign (1902) for 'Die
Fläche' a design magazine founded in 1900 by Bruno
Seuchter
Die Fläche 1, page 94: artistic writing by Bruno
Seuchter. Page 95: artistic writing by Anton Kling
(Vienna, 1881-Karlsruhe, Germany, 1963)

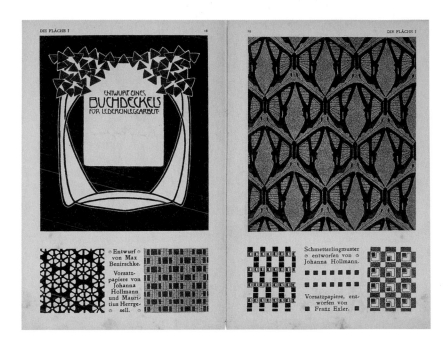

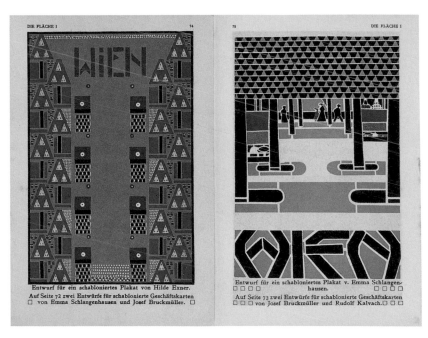

Die Fläche 1, pages 18 and 19: decorative designs by Max
Benirschke, Johanna Hollman, Mauritius Herrgesell and
Franz Exler

Die Fläche 1, page 74: design by Hilde Exner for a stencilled poster. Page 75: design by Emma Schlangenhausen
(Hall, Austria 1882-Grossgmain, Austria 1947) for a stencilled poster

Laskoff, Franz (Italy 1869-1918) c. 1901, Officine.
Ricordi & C., Milan. 202 x 144 cm, Italy

Krämer, Johann Victor (Austria 1861-Vienna 1949)
1901. 123.5 x 90 cm, Austria

WIENER KÜNSTLERBVND HAGEN

AVSSTELLVNG MÄRZ·1903

KVNSTSALON·RICHTER PRAGERSTRASZE

CHRISTOPH REISSER'S SÖHNE WIEN V.

Leffler, Heinrich (Austria, Vienna 1863-Vienna 1919)
1902/03, lithographic poster, 87.5 x 58 cm, Austria

Thorn Prikker, Johan (The Netherlands, The Hague 1888-Germany, Cologne 1932) 1903, Lith. S. Lankhout & Co., The Hague. 85 x 119 cm, The Netherlands (This copy of the poster was donated by the artist to the Vereniging tot Opvoeding en Verzorging van het Kind and is the original version. Later printings lack the background color.)

abcdefghijklmnopq

rstuvwxyz

1234567890

ABCDEFGHIJKLMN

OPQRSTUVWXYZ

.,-:;!?"'-(*[&%—

Morris Fuller Benton 1872-1948, USA. Engineer, type designer.

Fonts Century roman (with Theodor Low de Vinne, 1895), Alternate Gothic (1903), Franklin Gothic (1903-12), Cheltenham (1904), Clearface (1907), News Gothic (1908), Bodoni (1909), Cloister Oldstyle (1913), Souvenir (1914), Garamond (with T. M. Cleveland, 1914), Goudy bold, 1916, Century Schoolbook (1919), Civilité (1922), Broadway (1928), Bulmer (1928), Bank Gothic (1930), Stymie (with S. Hess and G. Powell, 1931), American Text (1932).

Franklin Gothic Produced by **ATF** in 1904.

Morris Fuller Benton's personal version of the

heavy sans serifs first made popular by **Vincent**

Figgins in 1830. Franklin Gothic remains popular

after nearly a hundred years of use.

79

ABab

ABCabc

ABCDabcd

gG
M

Junk, Rudolf (Austria, Vienna 1880-Rekawinkel, 1943)
front cover for the Hagenbund Spring 1907 exhibition
catalogue

Karpellus, Adolf (Austria 1869-Vienna 1919) 1907,
K. u. K. Hofl. J. Weiner, Vienna. 122 x 93 cm, Austria

Hohlwein, Ludwig (Germany, Wiesbaden 1874-Berchtes-
gaden 1949) 1908, Graph. Anstalt J. E. Wolfensberger,
Zürich. 122 x 92 cm, Germany

Hohlwein, Ludwig (Germany, Wiesbaden 1874-
Berchtesgaden 1949) 1911. Marco-Polo-Tee, Vereinigte
Druckereien und Kunstanstalten G.m.b.H. (G. Schuh &
Cie), München. 110 x 75.5 cm, Germany

Vereinigte Druckereien u.Kunstanstalten, G.m.b.H (Schuh & Co)-München,Herrnstr.15.

Hohlwein, Ludwig (Germany, Wiesbaden 1874-
Berchtesgaden 1949) 1909, 121 x 88.5 cm, Germany

Karpelius, F. (Austria) 1908. Jubiläumsausstellung
Künstlerhaus, K. u. K. Hofl. J. Weiner, Wien [od].
126 x 87.5 cm, Austria

Klinger, Julius (Austria, Vienna 1876-Vienna 1950)
1910, Hollerbaum & Schmidt, Berlin. 69 x 48 cm

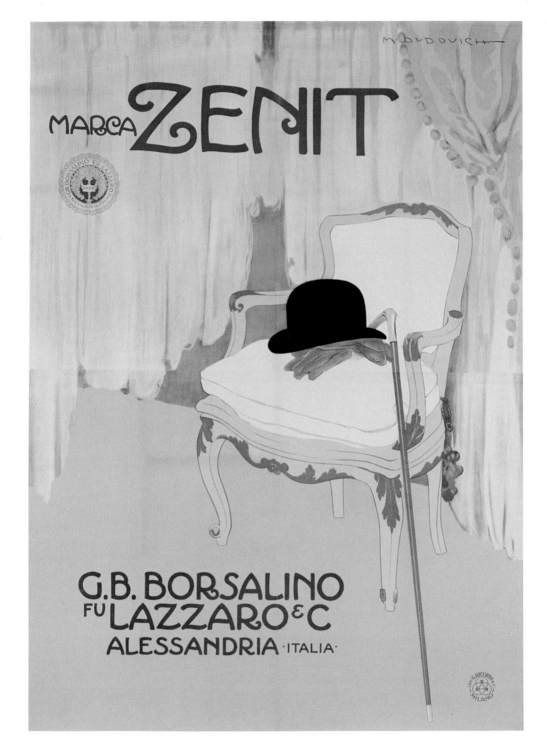

Dudovich, Marcello (Italy, Trieste 1878-Milan 1962)
1911, Officine G. Ricordi & C., Milan. 203 x 142.5 cm,
Italy

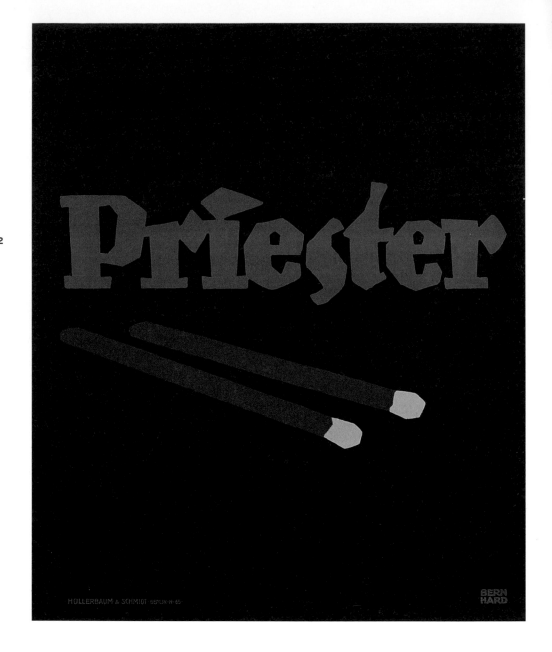

Bernhard, Lucian (Germany, Stuttgart 1883-USA,
New York 1972) c. 1910, Hollerbaum & Schmidt, Berlin
59.5 x 48.5 cm, Germany (This is the restyled version
of Bernhard's first poster design of 1903.)

Bernhard, Lucian (Germany, Stuttgart 1883-USA,
New York 1972) 1911, Hollerbaum & Schmidt, Berlin.
69.5 x 96 cm, Germany (The design represents ciga-
rettes brought back to the simplest form. Only
Raymond Loewy would create an even more abstract
design for Lucky Strike.)

94

Bernhard, Lucian (Germany, Stuttgart 1883-USA,
New York 1972) 1910, Hollerbaum & Schmidt, Berlin.
69.5 x 96 cm, Germany (Bernhard designed many
posters for the Manoli brand. Manoli being Ilona
Mandelbaum, wife of the owner of the company,
in reverse.)

Bernhard, Lucian (Germany, Stuttgart 1883-USA,
New York 1972) 1912, Hollerbaum & Schmidt, Berlin.
70 x 96 cm, Germany

Barrère, Adrien (France 1877-1931) 1912/3, Pathé
Frères Editeurs. 159.5 x 119.5 cm, France. (Prince
[Rigadin] was the first actor/comedian to reach film-
star-status. As a result it was sufficient to show his
well-known face on a poster promoting his films.)

Leffler, Heinrich (Austria, Vienna 1863-Vienna 1919)
c. 1917, lithographic poster

Lebeau, J.J. Chris (The Netherlands 1878-1945)
c. 1915, Litho Lankhout, The Hague. 125.5 x 89 cm,
The Netherlands

GRAPHIC

DESIGN

20TH

CENTURY

The Bauhaus opened in Weimar in 1919 with Walter Gropius becoming its first director and originator of its name. Goals included a unity of art and craft and utile designs with functional forms.

Schlemmer, Oskar (Germany 1888-1943), 1918.
65 x 51 cm, Germany. (This poster preludes the
Bauhaus, where Schlemmer would become one of
the first masters. To understand the importance
of this design it is good to realise that the First
World War was still being fought.)

102

van Anrooy, H.A. (The Netherlands, 1885-1964) 1918,
Lithographic wrappers for the magazine Wendingen,
litho Aart van Dobbenburgh, 33 x 33 cm, The
Netherlands

Krenek, C. (Austria) 1918. Staatslotterie. K.K. Hof- und
Staatsdruckerei. 63 x 48 cm, Germany

Bernhard, Lucian (Germany, Stuttgart 1883-USA, New York 1972) 1918, Werbedienst G.M.G.H., Berlin. Anschuss; der Frauenverbände Deutschlands. 68 x 95 cm, Germany. (The women liberation movement had been in full swing before World War I, but the shortage of men during the war did much to emancipate women. This poster was designed for the first elections in Germany open to women.)

In The Netherlands, De Stijl, one of many iconoclastic responses to the tragedy of World War I, was established in 1917 by Theo Van Doesburg and others including the architect J.J.P. Oud and the painters Vilmos Huszár and Piet Mondrian.

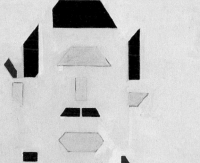

DELFTSCHE

SLA   OLIE

PLANTENVET

DELFIA

BvaLick'19

Fuchs, Heinz (Germany, Berlin 1886-Berlin 1961).
1919. 104 x 74 cm, Germany

Toorop, Jan Theodoor (Java 1858-The Hague 1928)
1919, S. Lankhout & Co, The Hague. 113 x 84.5 cm,
The Netherlands. (Because of the Spanish Flu that
terrorized Europe, public gatherings were to be avoided. As a result only a few proofs of this poster were
printed, since the performances for 'Pandorra' had to be
cancelled.)

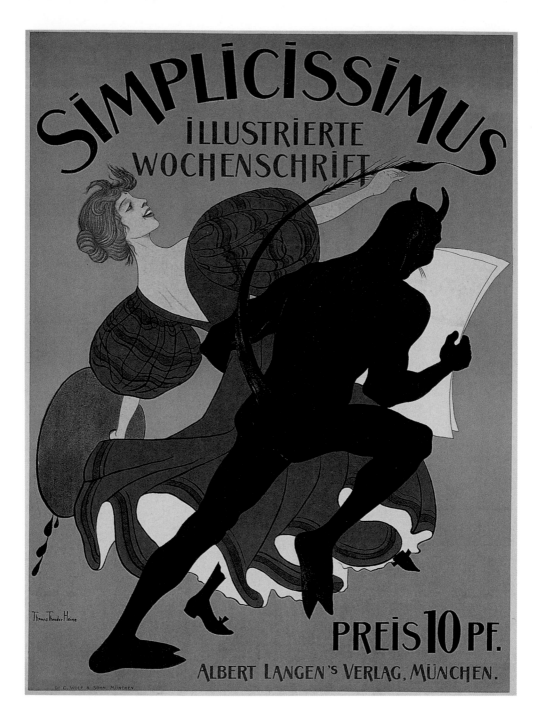

Heine, Thomas Theodor (Germany, Leipzig 1867-
Sweden, Stockholm 1948) 1919. Simplicissimus.
Illustrierte Wochenschrift. Wolf & Sohn, München.
83 x 61.5 cm, Germany

terriiBLE SOLEEIL FÉROOCE

SENTIMENTAL

aveu-
glant
de
larmes

sur les jeunes ex-
plorateurs trompés
par leurs femmes
maîtresses
solennité d'un cocu
sur la ligne de l'é-
quateur

aveu-
glé
de
larmes
rouges

Lettre d'une jolie femme
à un monsieur passéiste

CHAIR RRR

èÈÈÈÈÈÈÈèèèèèèèèèèèèèèèèèèèèèèèè
+ baisers + − X + + caresses + fraîcheur
beauté élégance 3000 frs. par mois
+ − + − X + + − + bague rubis 8000
vanitéeeeeeeeee + 6000 frs. chaus-
sures Demain chez toi Je suis serieuse
dévouée Tendresses

Marinetti, Filippo Achille Emilio (Filippo Tommaso)
(Egypt, Alexandria 1876-Italy, Bellagio 1944) pages 92
and 81 from his book 'Les mots en liberte futuristes'
published in 1919 by 'Poesia', Milan, Italy

Fenneker, Josef (Germany 1895-1956) 1920. 140 x 95 cm,
Germany

Klein, Cesar (Germany, Hamburg 1876-Pandorf
1954) 1919, Günther Wagner Hannover & Vienna.
61.5 x 50 cm, Germany

Fuss, Albert (Germany 1889-1969) 1920, Kunstanst.
Wüsten & Co., Frankfurt a/M 1920. 75 x 51 cm,
Germany

GRAPHIC

DESIGN

20TH

CENTURY

Graphic Design was an essential propaganda tool during World War I. Some of the British and American posters appealed to sentimentality. Others were more straightforward.

3 Worte:
Ungestörte Demobilmachung
Aufbau der Republik
Frieden

Jongert, Jacob (The Netherlands 1883-1942)
c. 1920. 1920. Druk Immig & Z. 100 x 75 cm,
The Netherlands

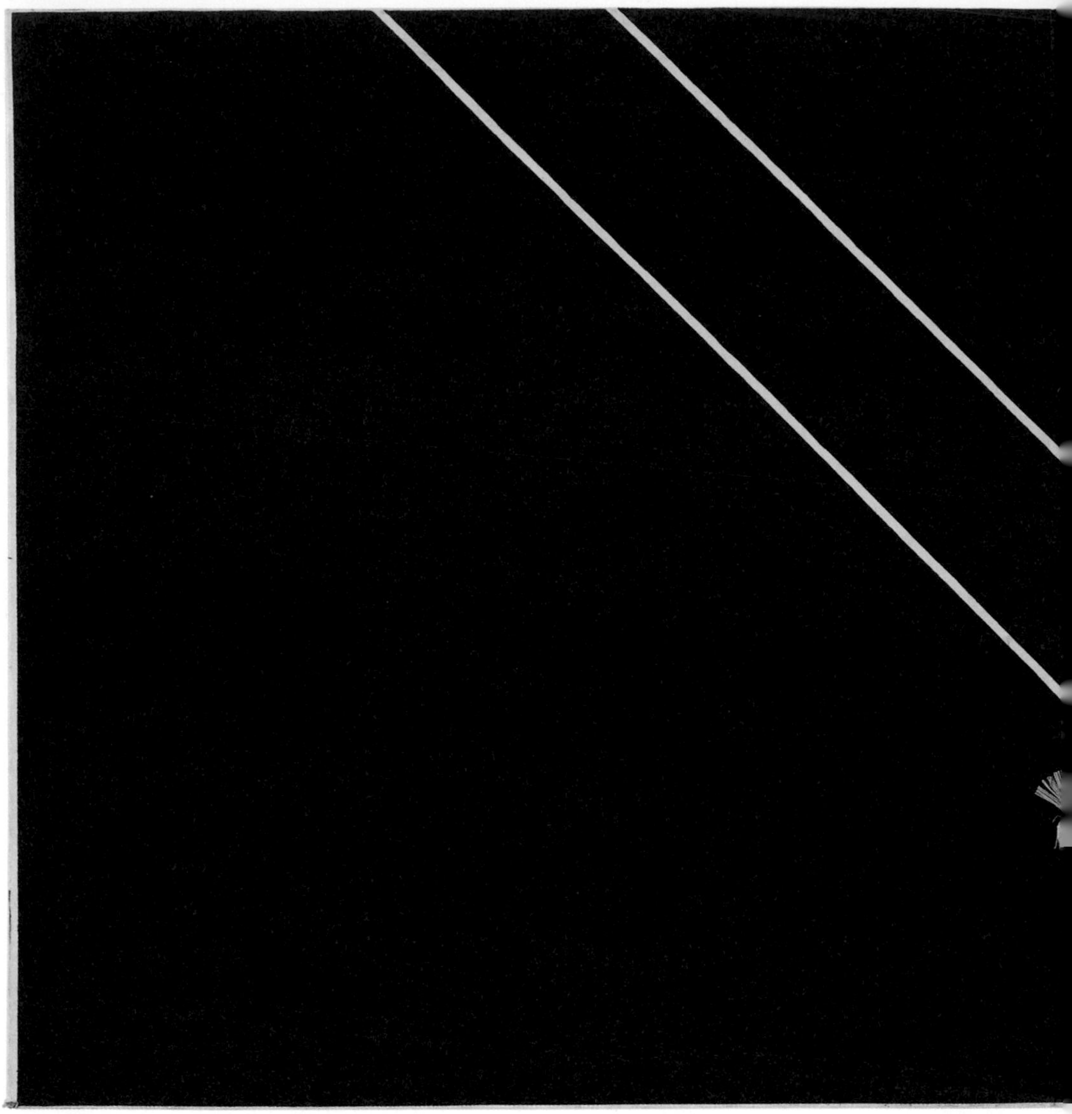

Bijvoet, B. (The Netherlands, Amsterdam 1889-
Amsterdam 1979) and **Duiker, J.** (The Netherlands,
The Hague 1890-Amsterdam 1935) 1921. Lithographic
wrappers for the magazine Wendingen, 33 x 33 cm,
The Netherlands

LETTERKLANKBEELDEN
DOOR I. K. BONSET

I

C
S
S
C
S-
Z'

Q
K
Q'
Q
Q'

R—
R-
o

103

O
X'

A—
H—
a—
h—
M— —

N
M
H

p'

II

Q-K **X'**

104

Q X
X'
m M **M M‾**
X'

III

Z' Z' Z' Z'
i _ _
Z' Z' Z'
i _ _
Z' Z'
i _ _
Z
a

p' p'
P P **P P P P P**

105

a
i _ _
X K M
X K M
X K M
Q_
Q' U'
U' Q'
f f f
K f_
O'
O_
H'
X R
Q K
Q R O i'
M _ _

106

Bonset, L.K. (pseud. Theo van Doesburg) (The
Netherlands, Utrecht 1883-Switzerland, Davos 1931)
1921. A poem Letterklankbeelden (Images of letter
sounds) De Stijl magazine vol. 4, no. 7, The
Netherlands

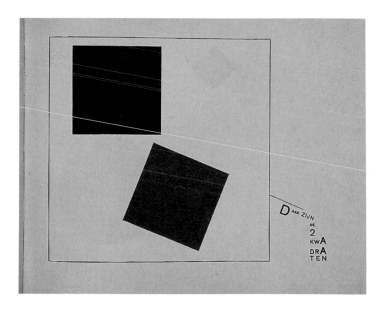

Lissitzky, Lazar Markovitch (El) (Russia, Pochinok 1890-USSR, Schodnia 1941) Front cover and page 3 of the Dutch edition of the Tale of Two Squares, letter-press, published by De Stijl, 1922

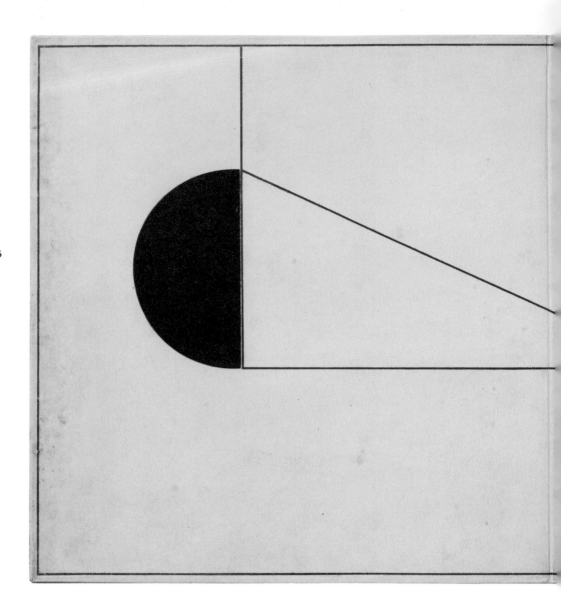

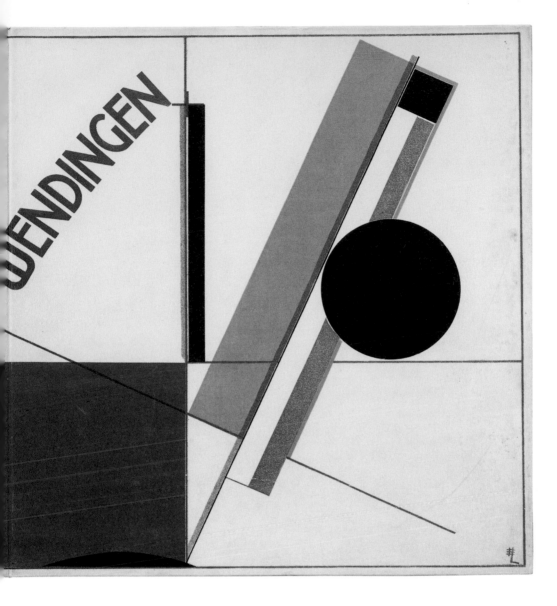

Lissitzky, Lazar Markovitch (El) (Russia, Pochinok
1890-USSR, Schodnia 1941) 1922, lithographic wrappers
for the magazine Wendingen, 33 x 33 cm, The
Netherlands

Sharing some of the objectives of Futurism, Dada began as a literary movement when the poet Hugo Ball started the Cabaret Voltaire in Zurich as a meeting place for young poets. Chance placement and absurd titles characterized their graphic work.

MERZ

1

DA
DA   DA
DA

HOLLAND

DADA

JANUAR 1923
HERAUSGEBER: KURT SCHWITTERS
HANNOVER · WALDHAUSENSTRASSE 5"

Wijdeveld, Hendrikus Theodorus (The Netherlands
1885-1987) 1923 letterpress

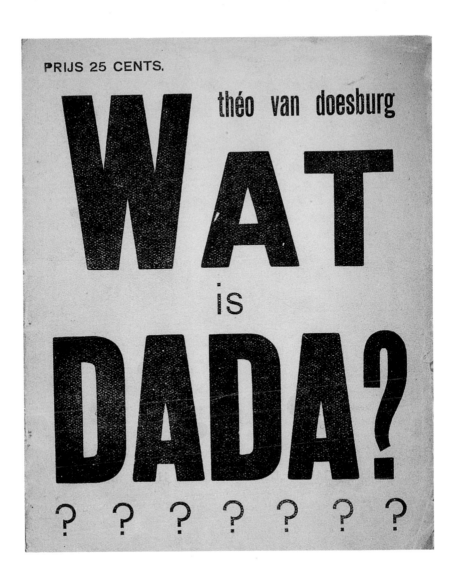

van Doesburg, Theo (The Netherlands, Utrecht 1883-
Switzerland, Davos 1931) 1923. Cover of the booklet
Wat is Dada? (What is Dada), De Stijl, The Netherlands

Lissitzky, Lazar Markovitch (EI) (Russia, Pochinok 1890-USSR, Schodnia 1941) front cover and pages 34/35 and 56/57 of his book 'Dlya Golosa'/ 'Zum Vorlesen', published in Berlin 1923

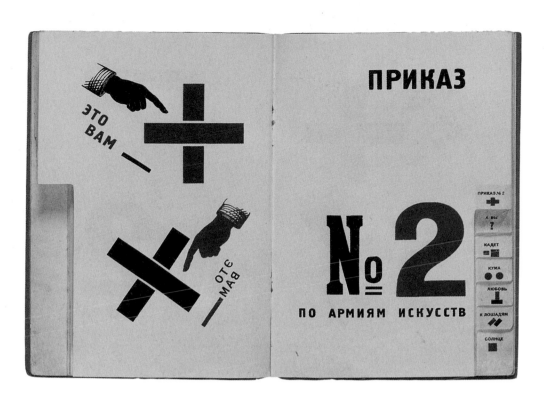

Schmidt, Joost (Germany 1893-1948) 1923, Reineck
& Klein, Weimar. 68 x 48 cm, Germany.
(The influence of Oskar Schlemmer, master at
The Bauhaus, is obvious. When, after several
postponements, the exhibition finally opened in
August 1923, the poster had to be altered.

Two pieces of paper were pasted on to show the
correct dates, and usually it is this altered version
that is shown in books on the Bauhaus. This copy
is from the collection of Dr. Adolf Behne, who dis-
cussed and illustrated it in the Dutch monthly
De Reclame of November 1923.)

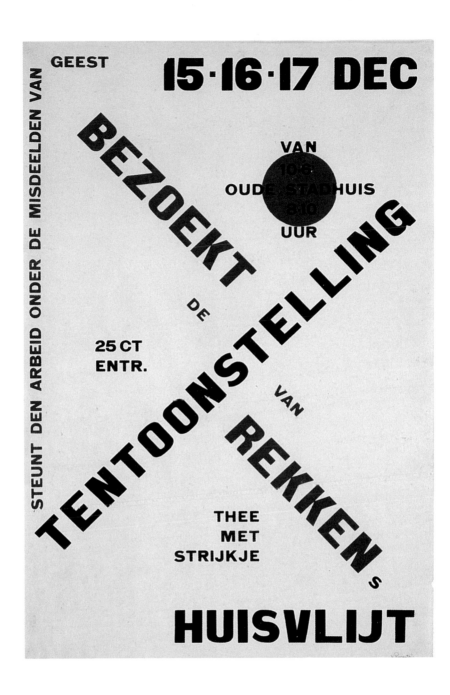

van Ravesteyn, Sybold (The Netherlands
1889-1983) c.1925, letterpress. 98.5 x 64 cm,
The Netherlands. (When asked why he designed
this poster the way he did, Van Ravesteyn,
an architect by profession, answered: 'It was
just the whim of the time.')

Art Deco was the popular international style during the 1930s. Although it can be seen as a last extension of Art Nouveau, its geometric-based forms reflect Cubism, Futurism, and Dada.

Stenberg Brothers Georgi (Russia 1900-USSR 1933)
and **Vladimir Augustovich Stenberg** (Moscow 1899-
Moscow 1982) and **Konstantin Medunetsky** (1899-
1935) 1923. 72 x 47 cm, France

Polet, Johan (1894-1971) 1923. Lithographic wrappers for the magazine Wendingen, 33 x 33 cm, The Netherlands

KUBISMUS / **CUBISME** / **CUBISM**

CUBISM

What distinguishes cubism from precedent painture is this: not to be an art of imitation but a conception that tends to rise itself as creation. APOLLINAIRE.

Instead of the impressionist illusion of space based on the perspective of air and the naturalism of colour, cubism offers the simpel and abstracted forms in their precise relations of character and measure. ALLARD.

FUTURISMUS / **FUTURISME** / **FUTURISM**

FUTURISM

Futurists have abolished quietness and stalism and have demonstrated movement, dynamism. They have documented the new conception of space by confrontation of interior and exterior.

For us gesture will not any more be a fixed moment of universal dynamism! It will decidedly be the dynamic sensation eternalised as such. BOCCIONI.

EXPRESSIONISMUS / **EXPRESSIONISME** / **EXPRESSIONISM**

EXPRESSIONISM

From cubism and futurism has been chopped the minced meat, the mystic german beefsteak: expressionism.

142

ABSTRAKTE KUNST / **ART ABSTRAIT** / **ABSTRACT ART**

ABSTRACT ART

The abstract artists give form to the inobjective without being bound by a common problem. Abstractivism offers multiple senses.

METAPHYSIKER / **MÉTAPHYSICIENS** / **METAPHYSICIANS**

METAPHYSICIANS

To represent the immaterial by the material is the problem of the metaphysicians. As futurists they would put fire to the museums, as metaphysicians they are happy to use museums as asylums for the old age. This is the punishment for having wished to measure eternity with three cowstails.

SUPREMATISMUS / **SUPRÉMATISME** / **SUPREMATISM**

SUPREMATISM

Midnight of art is ringing. Fine art is banished. The artist-idol is a prejudice of the past. Suprematism presses the entire painture into a black square on a white canvas.

'I did not invent anything. It's only the night I felt in me, and it is there I perceived the new, which I called suprematism. It has expressed itself by the black plain that formed a square.' MALEWITSCH.

By the inflation of the square the art-exchanges have procured the means to deal in art to everybody. Now the production of works of art is judiciously so facilitated and simplified that nobody

Lissitzky, Lazar Markovitch (El) (Russia, Pochinok 1890–USSR, Schodnia 1941) pages VIII/IX and 18/19 of the book 'Kunstismen 1914-1924' by El Lissitzky and Hans Arp published in 1925 by Eugen Rentsch Verlag in Erlenbach-Zürich, Switzerland

3

46

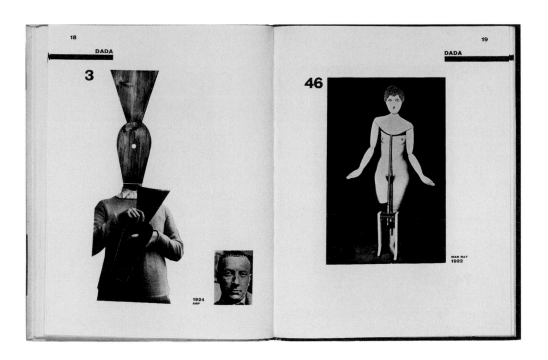

1924
ARP

MAN RAY
1922

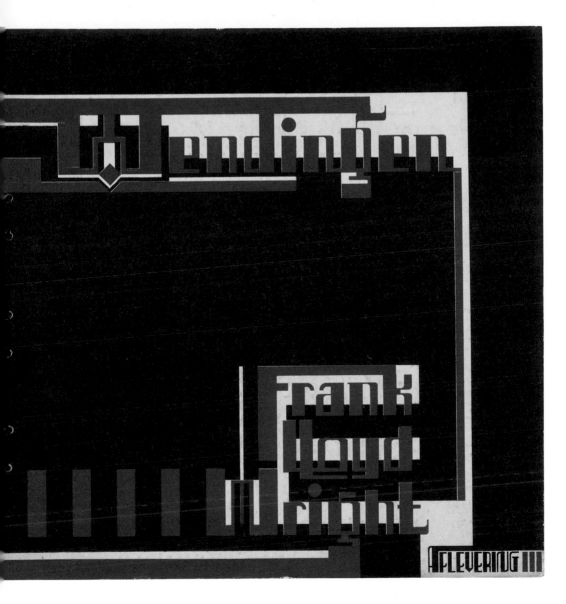

Wijdeveld, Hendrikus Theodorus (The Netherlands,
The Hague 1885-1987) 1925, Lithographic wrappers for
the magazine Wendingen, 33 x 33 cm, The Netherlands

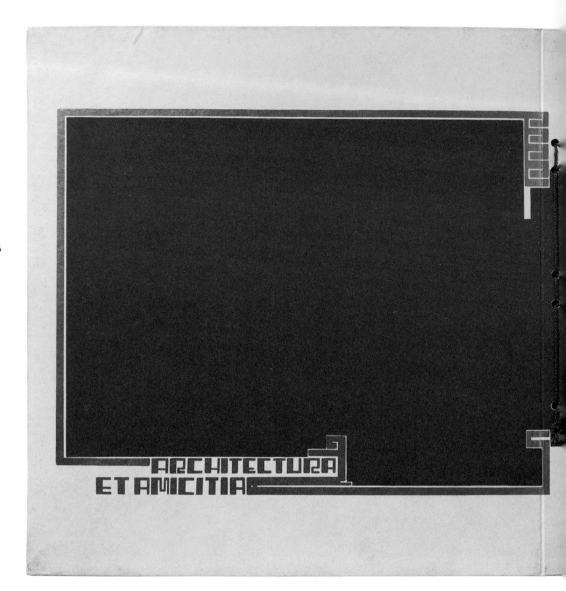

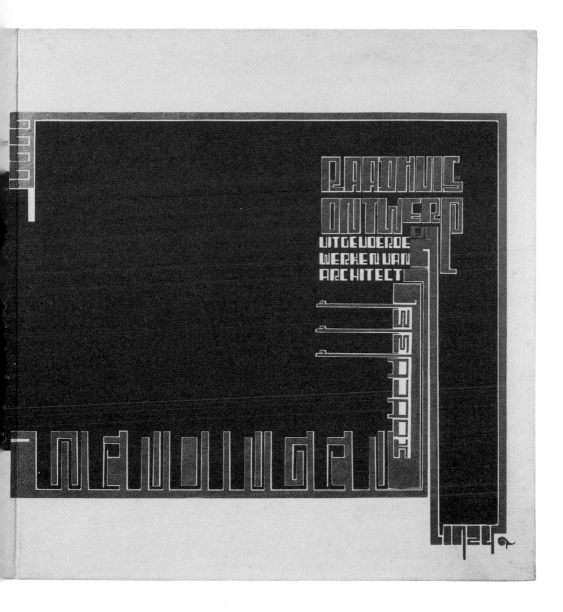

Dudok, Willem Marinus (The Netherlands, Amsterdam 1884-1974) 1924, Lithographic wrappers for the magazine Wendingen, 33 x 33 cm, The Netherlands

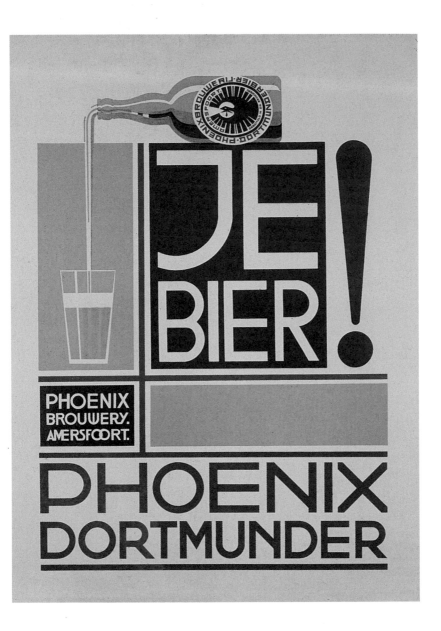

de Koo, Nicolaas Petrus (The Netherlands 1881-1960)
c. 1924. 67 x 49 cm, The Netherlands

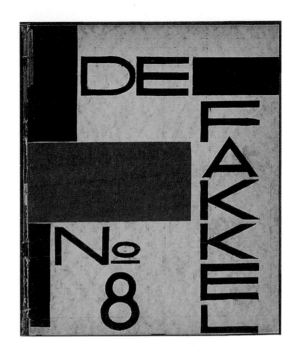

Schuitema, G. Paul H. (The Netherlands 1897-1973)
front cover (woodcut) for the January 1926 issue of
the monthly 'de Fakkel'

E STYLE - DER STIL - THE STILE -

OUVELLE CONSCIENCE PLASTIQUE ET POÉTIQUE FONDÉ EN 1917 EN HOLLAND

PÉRIODIQUE
DRUKWERKEN

van Doesburg, Theo (The Netherlands, Utrecht 1883-
Switzerland, Davos 1931) Cover of the magazine De
Stijl, letterpress, issues 75/76, 1926

Mailing wrapper of the magazine De Stijl, letterpress,
c. 1924

152

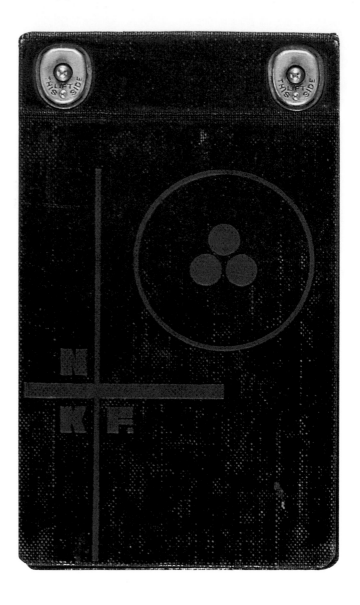

Zwart, Piet (The Netherlands, Zaandijk 1885-
Leidschendam, 1977). 1926, front cover and four pages
of a calendar booklet with information on wirecables
produced by the Netherlands Cable Works Ltd (NKF)

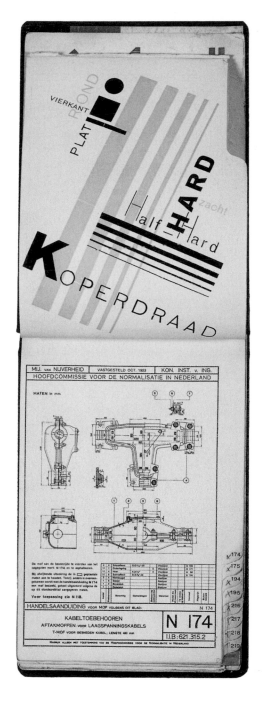

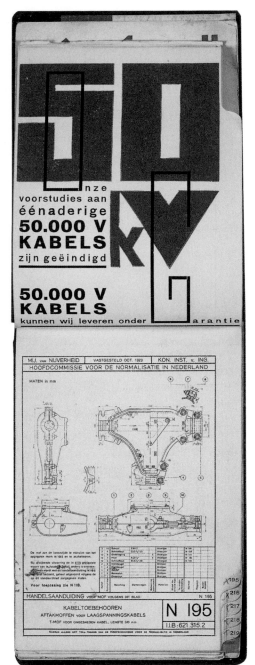

**Kurt Schwitters, Käte Steinitz, and Theo van
Doesburg** page 9 from 'die Scheucke' (the scarecrow)
letterpress published as Merz issue 14/15 by Aposs
Verlag, Hannover 1925

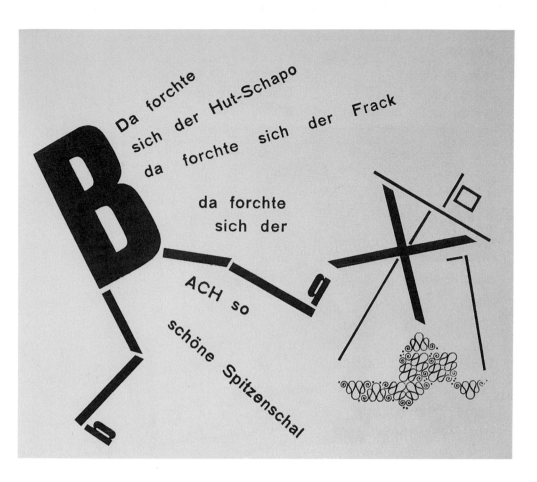

NN 1926 (?). 105 x 69.5 cm, Russia

Proussakov, Nikolai P. (Russia 1900-USSR 1952) and
Borisov, Grigorii Ilich (Russia 1899-1942) (A journey
to Mars) 1926. 101.5 x 73 cm, USSR

Tschichold, Jan (Germany, Leipzig 1902-
Switzerland, Locarno 1974), 1927, (for the film
Camille) 118.5 x 84 cm. To make sure that the ink of
the photo would stick on the paper and would not
blur the image, the paper was covered with a thin
layer of white powder.

Tschichold, Jan (Germany, Leipzig 1902-
Switzerland, Locarno 1974), 1927. 118.5 x 84 cm,
Germany

160

Tschichold, Jan (Germany, Leipzig 1902-
Switzerland, Locarno 1974), c. 1927. 118.5 x 84 cm

Tschichold, Jan (Germany, Leipzig 1902-
Switzerland, Locarno 1974). Photolitho and linocut
by Kunst im Druck GmbH, Munich, 1928. 119.5 x 85 cm

Müller, Carl Otto (Germany 1901-1970) c. 1927,
Linoleumschnitt u. -druck Münchner Plakatdruckerei
Volk & Schreiber, Munich. 119 x 85 cm, Germany

C.O. MÜLLER

Bayer, Herbert (Austria, Haag 1900-USA, Aspen 1985)
1927, Buch -u. Kunstdruckerei Ernst Hedrich Nachf.
Leipzig. 90 x 60 cm, Germany

Baumberger, Otto (Switzerland, Altstetten 1889-1961)
1928. 128 x 90 cm, Switzerland. (The Forster company
sold floor coverings which were stored in rolls.)

Stenberg Brothers Georgi (Russia 1900-USSR 1933) and
Vladimir Augustovich Stenberg (Moscow 1899-Moscow
1982) c. 1927. 105.5 x 76 cm, USSR. (French film: The Miracle
of the Wolves.)

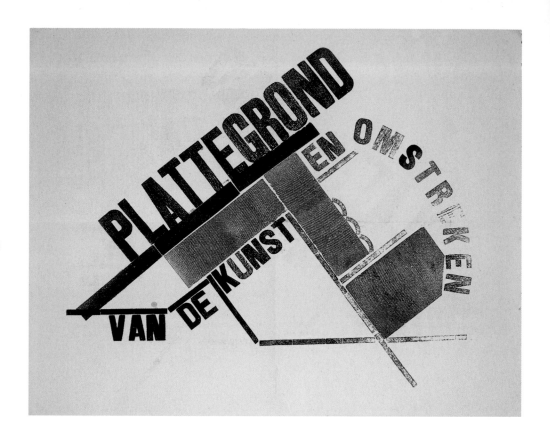

Werkman, Hendrik Nicolaas (The Netherlands, Leens
1882-Bakkeveen 1945) 1924. Cover and four-page cen-
terfold from The Next Call, no. 6, The Netherlands

In der Heftigkeit von Farben,
der Spontaneität
und im Wagemut
haben wir neue Freude und Kraft gefunden.
Ehrlichkeit, Entschlossenheit,
unerbittlicher Ernst
(auch in Fröhlichkeit)
Selbstzwang, Selbstkenntniss, Selbstkritik
sind Bausteine für die neue Stadt.

GLAS, EISEN, BETON.

Alles was das Licht scheut
krank ist oder sentimental oder
verfault, oder tot geboren, oder
alt geboren,
alle Schöntuerei und falsche Trücs
werden wir AUS UNSERER MITTE
FERN HALTEN.

Wir hassen
das Publikum, das keine Neuerung duldet,
keine Experimente, keine Evolution, keine Irrtümer.

Wir hassen
das Publikum, das den Künstler erniedrigt
zu einem Circus Artisten,
die Wiederholung seines Kunststückes fordernd
bis ins Endlose.

Wir hassen das Publikum,
das den Künstler zwingt seinen Geist auszubeuten,
ihn verwirft und ruft um etwas anderes.
Wir hassen das Publikum, das Kunst PROTEGIERT.

**Protektion: Krankheit der Kunst.
Akademie: Verderben der Kunst.
PRIX DE ROME: TOD der KUNST.**

Die ZEIT spricht!

Ebent

die Strassen und Wege
dass AUTO's durchjagen können
in fliegender Eile!
DRESCHMASCHINEN dröhnen in den Scheunen,
sacht sumsen die DYNAMO's wie Bienen in ihrem Korb,
im Feld klappern MÄHMASCHINEN,
die ANTENNE fängt jedes Erzittern des Æthers
auf ihren empfindlichen Saiten,
über uns, in der strahlenden Frühlingsluft
kreist der blinkende ÆROPLAN.
AUTO's werfen ihre Lichter zu den Wolken
der Schall der CLAXONS verfolgt uns in der Stille.

Nachtstädte, Lichtstädte!
Helle, neue Dörfer,
Fabriken, Kanäle, eisenklingende Werften,
wogende Drähte fliegender Signale,
die SONNE strahlt LEBEN in die Kupferdrähte,
der Wind singt in den Saiten.

Fort

mit den alten dumpfen Häusern,
wo der Staub von Jahrhunderten ruht
Malt die Wände rot, gelb oder orange
Lasst die Häuser brennen
von Farbe und Wœrme!

169

Werkman, Hendrik Nicolaas (The Netherlands, Leens
1882-Bakkeveen 1945) 1927. Pages of a compilation
De Ploeg Groningen, Holland, The Netherlands

Werkman, Hendrik Nicolaas (The Netherlands, Leens
1882-Bakkeveen 1945) front and back cover of the
Next Call 4, letterpress, designed and printed by
H.N. Werkman, Groningen (The Netherlands) 1924

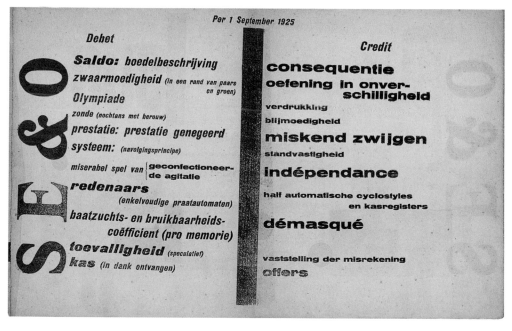

Werkman, Hendrik Nicolaas (The Netherlands, Leens 1882-Bakkeveen 1945) front cover and middle pages of the Next Call 8, letterpress, designed and printed by H.N. Werkman, Groningen (The Netherlands) 1925

abcdefghijklmnopq

rstuvwxyz

1234567890

ABCDEFGHIJKLMN

OPQRSTUVWXYZ

.,-:;!?''-(*[&%—

Paul Renner 1878-1956, Germany. Graphic artist, painter, type designer, author, teacher.

Fonts Futura (1928), Plak (1928), Futura Black (1929), Futura licht (1932), Futura Schlagzeile (1932), Ballade (1937), Renner Antiqua (1939), Steile Futura (1952).

Futura Is the fully developed prototype of the twentieth-century Geometric Sans serif. The form is ancient. Greek capitals were inscribed by the Cretans 2500 years ago at the time of Pythagoras in the Cortyn Code, by the Imperial Romans, notably in the tomb of the Scipios; by classical revival architects in eighteenth-century London, who created the basis for **Caslon's** first sans-serif typeface in 1817. Some aspects of the geometric sans serif survived in the flood of Gothics that followed, particularly in the work of **Vincent Figgins**.

In 1927, stimulated by the Bauhaus experiments in geometric form and the **Ludwig & Mayer** typeface **Erbar, Paul Renner** sketched a set of Bauhaus forms; working from these, the professional letter design office at **Bauer** reinvented the sans serif based on strokes of even weight, perfect circles, and isosceles triangles and brought the Universal Alphabet and Erbar to their definitive typographic form. Futura became the most popular sans serif of the middle years of the twentieth century.

FUTURA FUTURA **FUTURA** FUTURA **FUTURA**

FUTURA **FUTURA** FUTURA **FUTURA**

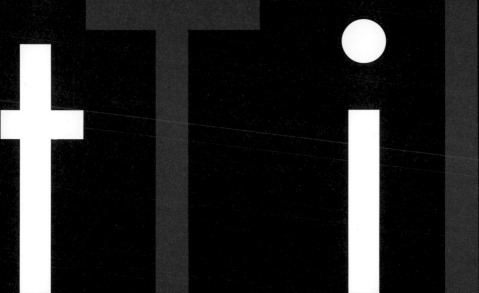

Gispen, W.H. (The Netherlands, Amsterdam 1890-The
Hague 1981) 1928, Lithographic wrappers for the
magazine Wendingen, 33 x 33 cm, The Netherlands

Huszar, Vilmos (Hungary, Budapest 1884-The
Netherlands, Harderwijk 1960) 1929 lithographic cover
for the monthly 'de Reclame'

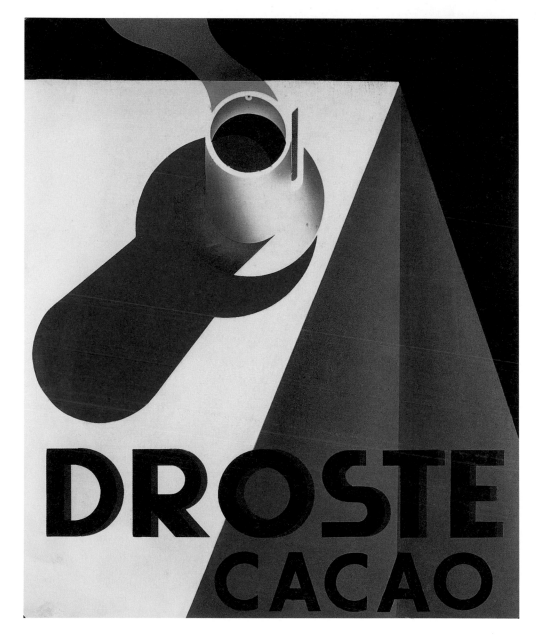

Cassandre, A.M. (pseudonym for Adolphe Jean-Marie
Mouron) (Poland, Krakau 1901-France, Paris 1968).
1929, 96.5 x 116 cm, enamel sign produced by the firm
Langcat, Bussum, The Netherlands

Wijdeveld, Hendrikus Theodorus (The Netherlands 1885-
1987) 1929, letterpress. 65 x 51 cm, The Netherlands

Cassandre, A.M. (pseudonym for Adolphe Jean-Marie Mouron) (Poland, Krakau 1901-France, Paris 1968) 1929 front cover and pages 4/5 of a promotional booklet for the 'Bifur', a letter designed by A.M. Cassandre, printed by Deberny Peignot, Paris

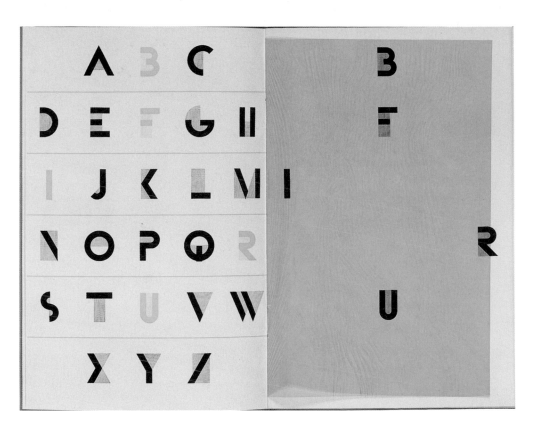

Domela, Cesar (The Netherlands, Amsterdam 1900-
France, Paris 1992) c. 1928. Cover of a prospectus for
the progressive Juute Klamt Dance School, Berlin,
Germany

GEBR. FRETZ AG. ZURICH

kunsthaus zürich
abstrakte und
surrealistische malerei
und plastik

6.oktober bis 3.november 1929 täglich geöffnet 10-12 und 2-5 montags geschlossen

Arp, Jean (Hans) (Alsace, Strassburg 1887-
Switzerland, Basel 1966) and **Cyliax, Walter**
(Germany, Leipzig 1899- Vienna 1945) 1928 lithograph
by Gebr. Fretz AG, Zürich

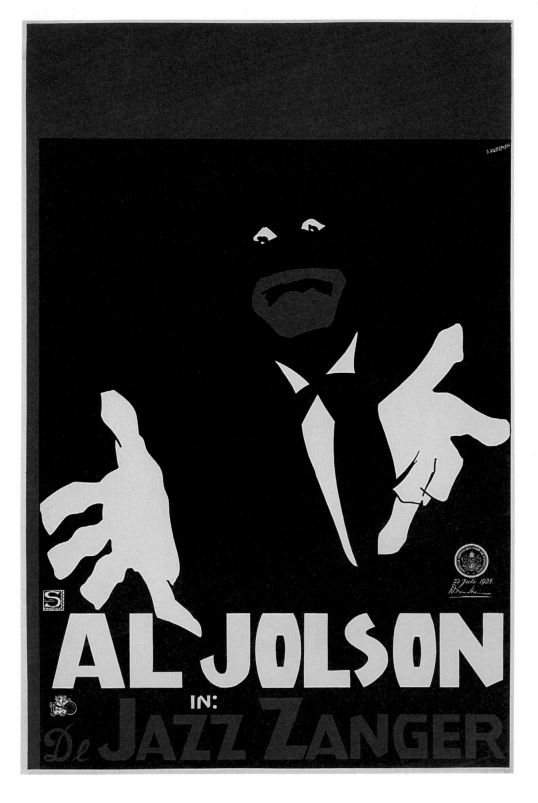

Rüdeman, Gustave Adolphine Wilhelmina
(Dolly Rudeman) (Java 1902-Amsterdam 1980)
1928, Strang & Co, The Hague. 92.5 x 60.5 cm,
Netherlands. (The Jazz Singer starring Al Jolson
was the first talking picture. The design
was adapted from the original American
promotional material designed by William
Auerbach-Levy.)

Zwart, Piet (The Netherlands, Zaandijk 1885-Leidschendam, 1977). 1929 booklet published by the Dutch postal services with information on airmail services to the Dutch East Indies (Indonesia)

Fototek 1   Klinkhardt & Biermann   Verlag-Publishers-Editeurs   Berlin W 10

Moholy-Nagy, László (Hungary 1895-1946) 1930 front
cover for Fototek 1, published by Klinkhardt &
Biermann, Berlin 1930

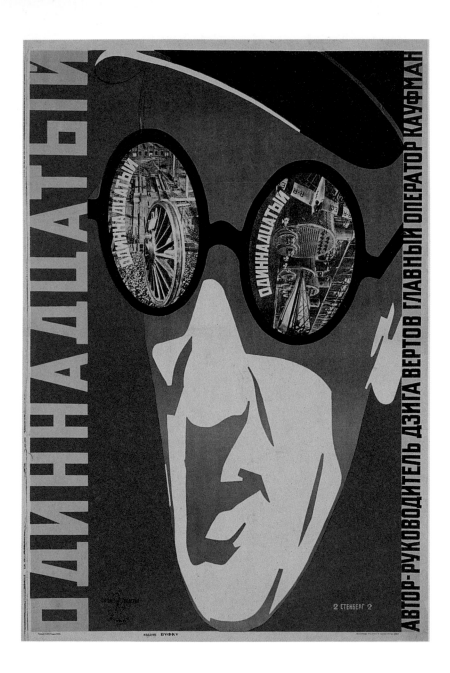

Stenberg Brothers Georgi (Russia 1900-USSR 1933)
and **Vladimir Augustovich Stenberg** (Moscow 1899-
Moscow 1982) 1928. 104.6 x 70.7 cm, USSR. (Soviet
film: The Eleventh Year of the Revolution.)

NN 1927. Sovkino Moskou.

Zwart, Piet (The Netherlands, Zaandijk 1885-
Leidschendam 1977) 1928, M.V. v/h I Strang & Co&'s
Drukkerijen, The Hague. 108 x 78 cm, The Netherlands

Gispen, Willem Hendrik (The Netherlands,
Amsterdam 1890-The Hague 1981) 1928, Kühn en Zn,
Rotterdam. 100 x 71 cm, The Netherlands

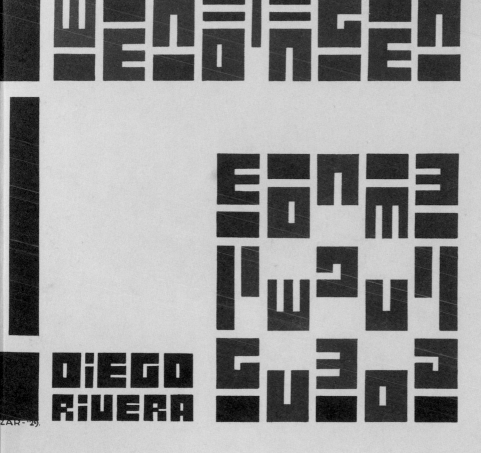

Huszar, Vilmos (Hungary, Budapest 1884-The Netherlands,
Harderwijk 1960) 1929, lithographic wrappers for the magazine Wendingen, 33 x 33 cm, The Netherlands

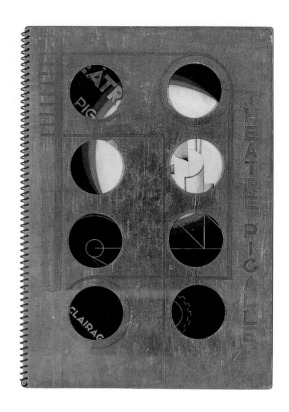

Carlu, Jean George Leon (France, Bonnières-sur-
Seine 1900-Paris 1997) 1929 cover, front page and
pages 6/7 from a promotional booklet for the Theatre
Pigalle

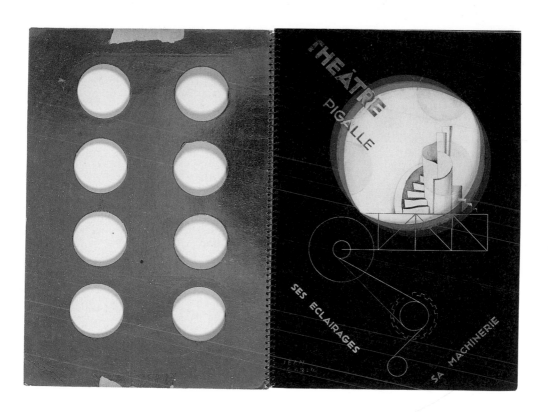

LE THÉATRE PIGALLE

Dans ce coin vibrant et grouillant de Paris, d'un attrait si particulier parce qu'il marque le seuil de la butte fameuse à laquelle l'esprit et l'art français ont attaché un immortel renom, nous sommes encore quelques Parisiens qui avons connu des oasis de verdure et de silence, jardins oubliés dans l'évolution progressive de la grande cité. L'un d'eux surtout ajoutait à son charme celui d'évoquer des souvenirs précieux : il avait abrité la « folie » que l'intendant Weymerange avait offerte à Adeline Colombe, la volage fauvette du Théâtre Italien; Scribe l'avait plus tard habité, et sous les ombrages de ses bosquets, la "Dame Blanche" avait rencontré "Haydée"; les "Huguenots" avaient en vers de huit pieds prêté serment à l'Amiral de Coligny, Bertrand s'était montré plus malicieux que Raton, et la "Favorite" avait croisé le "Prophète". Un beau jour pourtant, ces ombres illustres s'enfuirent, les moineaux prirent leur vol; les lauriers étaient coupés, les arbres tombèrent; du sol de ce jardin romantique surgit une construction

LE PÉRISTYLE

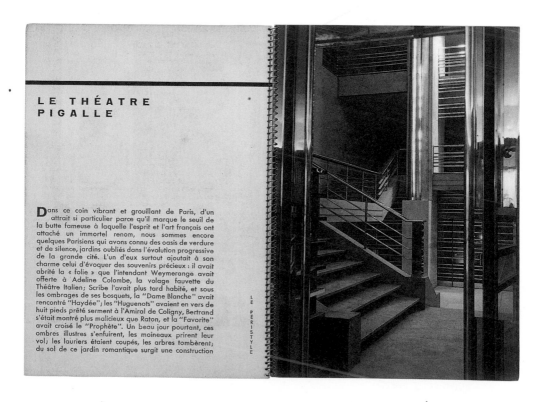

abcdefghijklmnopqr

stuvwxyz

1234567890

ABCDEFGHIJKLMN

OPQRSTUVWXYZ

.,-:;!?''-(*[&%—

Eric Gill 1882-1940, England. Sculptor, graphic artist, type designer. Studied at the Chichester Technical and Art School.

Fonts Gill Sans (1927-30), Golden Cockerell Roman (1929), Perpetua (1929-30), Solus (1929), Joanna (1930-31), Aries (1932), Floriated Capitals (1932), Bunyan, Pilgrim (1934), Jubilee (1934).

Gill Sans Gill's roots can be traced back to Old Face typefaces and more directly to Eric Gill's teacher Edward Johnston's London Underground type. Gill has such similarly proportioned strokes that the eye cannot tell the difference. This font exudes a modern feel due to its clear, generous, and original characters.

199

agpst

agpst

Carlu, Jean George Leon (France, Bonnières-sur-Seine 1900-Paris 1997) 1929, Imp.S.to A me Corbet, Paris 155 x 105 cm, France

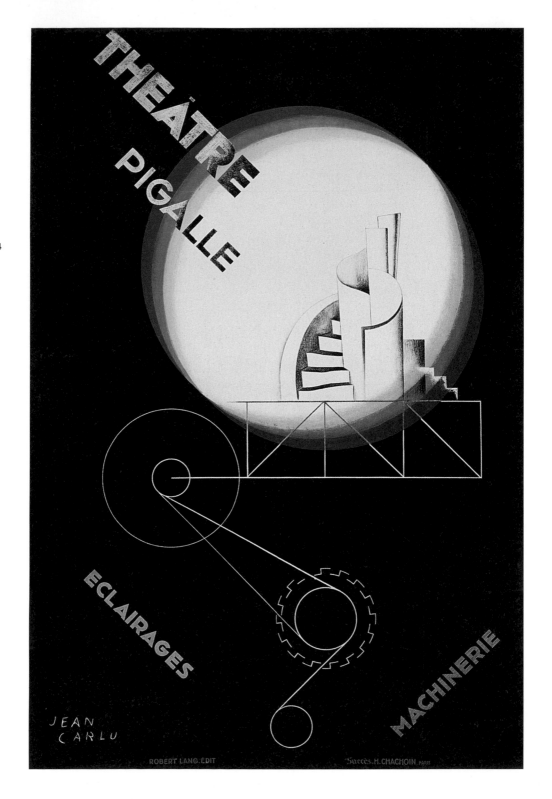

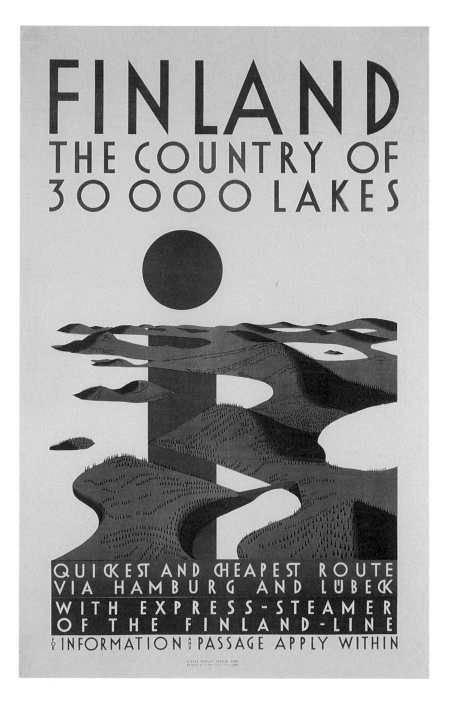

Carlu, Jean George Leon (France, Bonnières-sur-Seine 1900-Paris 1997) 1929, Succes H. Chachoin, Paris Robert Lang Édit. 1929. 155 x 102 cm, France

Mahlau, Alfred (Germany, Berlin 1894-Hamburg 1967) 1929, H.G. Rahtgens, GmbH, Lübeck. 101 x 62 cm, Germany

GRAPHIC

DESIGN

20TH

CENTURY

Always maintaining an uncomplicated approach to his work, Paul Colin became the most prolific French graphic designer of his generation.

Colin, Paul (France, 1892-1986) André Renaud 1929,
poster, Succes, H. Chachoin, Paris, 159 x 113 cm, France

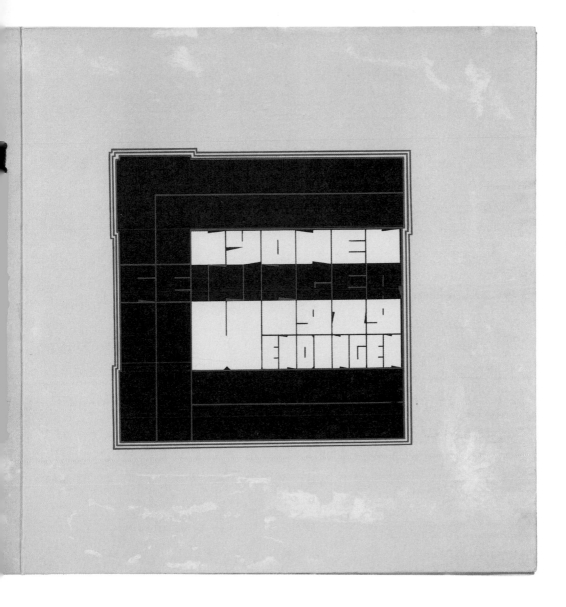

Baanders, Tine (The Netherlands, 1890-1971) 1929,
lithographic wrappers for the magazine Wendingen,
33 x 33 cm, The Netherlands

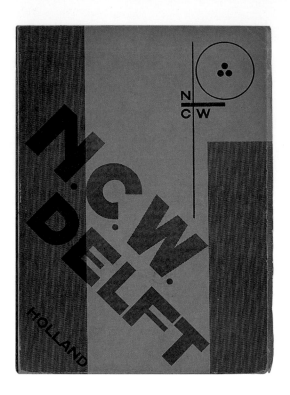

Zwart, Piet (The Netherlands, Zaandijk 1885-
Leidschendam, 1977) 1929. Pages 14/15 and front cover
of his catalogue (English edition) for the Netherlands
Cable Works Ltd (NKF)

Copper Wire

according to british standard and special requirements

tinned-Wire
Copper-**W**ire
Copper-cable

14

15

211

Copier, A. D. (1901-1991) 1930, lithographic wrappers for
the magazine Wendingen, 33 x 33 cm, The Netherlands

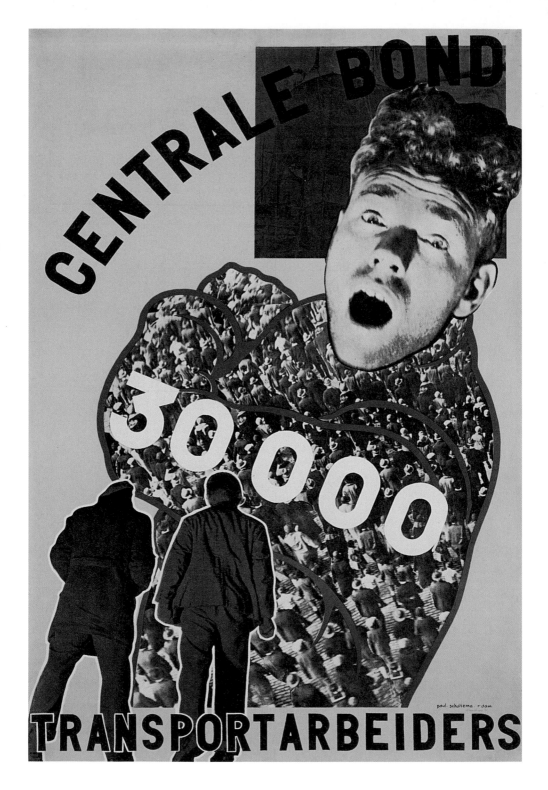

Schuitema, G. Paul H. (The Netherlands 1897-1973)
1930, 115.5 x 75.5 cm, The Netherlands

Stoecklin, Niklaus (Switzerland, Basel 1896-Riehen
1982) 1930, Art. Institut Orell Füssli, Zürich.
128 x 90 cm, Switzerland

Domela, Cesar (The Netherlands, Amsterdam 1900-
France, Paris 1992) c. 1930. Brochure for Diesel engine
trains, Ornstein & Koppel AG, Berlin, Germany

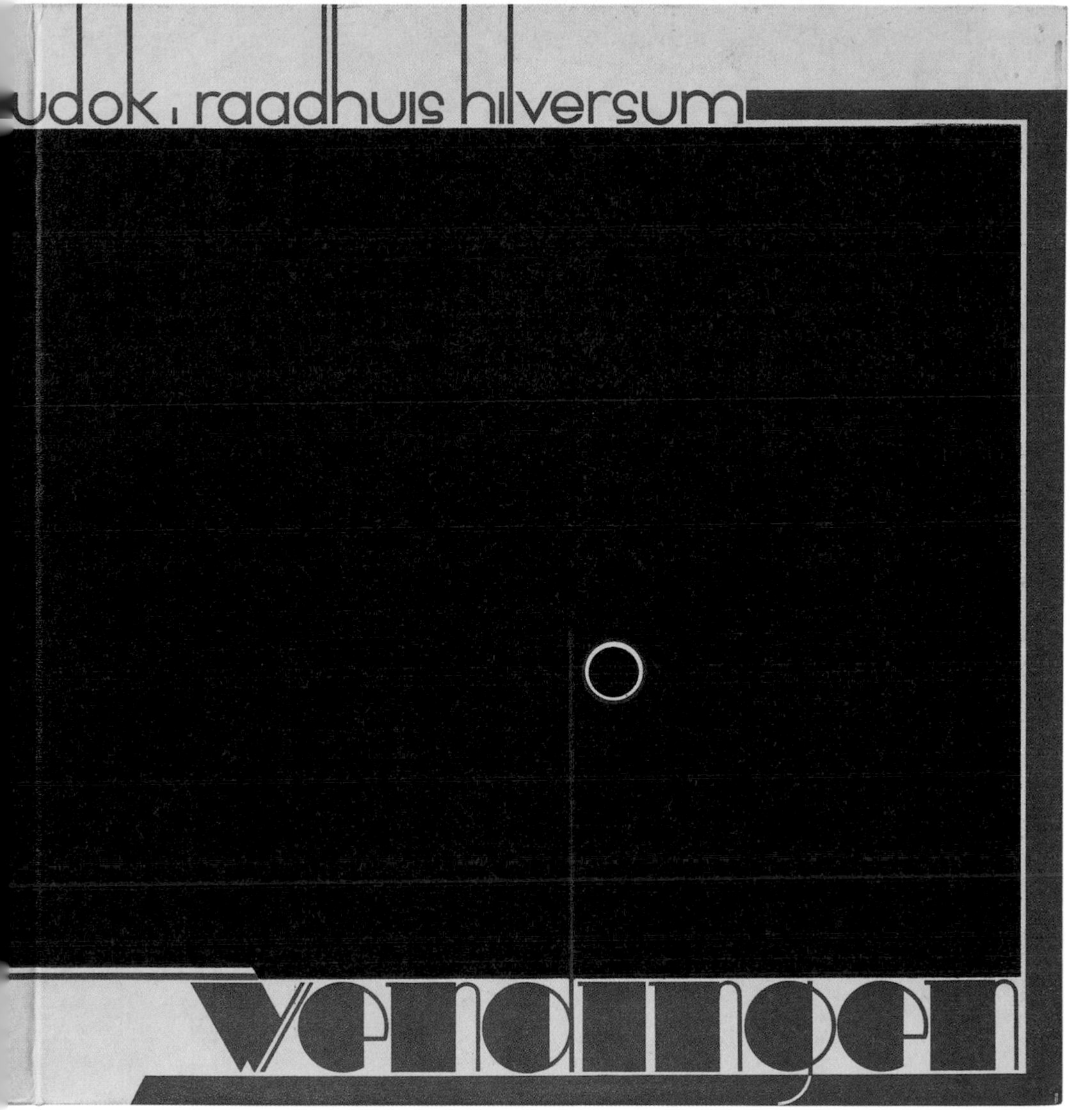

Dudok, Willem Marinus (The Netherlands, Amsterdam 1884-1974) 1930, Lithographic wrappers for the magazine Wendingen, 33 x 33 cm, The Netherlands

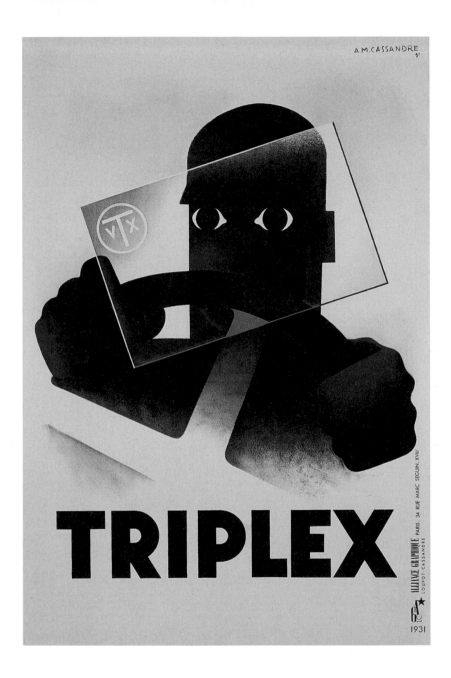

Cassandre, A.M. (pseudonym for Adolphe Jean-Marie
Mouron) (Poland, Krakau 1901-France, Paris 1968) 1927,
Hachard & Cie., Paris. 105 x 75.5 cm, France
(In 1928 the Olympics were to be held in Amsterdam
and this poster was meant to promote transportation
by rail to get there.)

Cassandre, A.M. (pseudonym for Adolphe Jean-Marie
Mouron) (Poland, Krakau 1901-France, Paris 1968) 1931,
Alliance Graphique Loupot-Cassandre, Paris. 120 x 80
cm, France

GRAPHIC

DESIGN

20TH

CENTURY

Fervently embracing the modern age, the Italian Futurists discarded old notions of harmony as they expressed speed and movement in visual design.

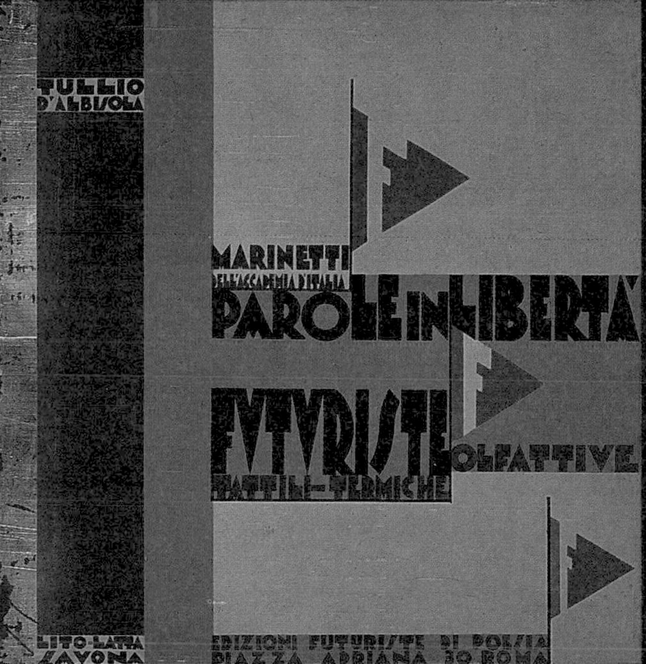

TULLIO
D'ALBISOLA

MARINETTI
DELL'ACCADEMIA D'ITALIA

PAROLE IN LIBERTÀ

FUTURISTE OLFATTIVE

TATTILI-TERMICHE

22

LITO-LATTA
SAVONA

EDIZIONI FUTURISTE DI POESIA
PIAZZA ADRIANA 30 ROMA

Marinetti, Filippo Achille Emilio (Filippo Tommaso)
(Alexandria, Egypt 1876-Bellagio, Italy, 1944) 1932, four
pages from his futurist book 'Parole in Liberta' printed
on metal

Schawinsky, Alexander (Xanti) (Switzerland, Basel
1904-Locarno 1979) 1934, Incisione e stampa S.A.
Alfieri e Lacroix, Milan. 96.5 x 66.5 cm, Italy

rijks-serietoestellen

de nieuwe uitvoering
met eenvoudige bediening
en vele mogelijkheden

Kiljan, Gerard (The Netherlands, Hoorn 1891-
Leidschendam 1968) c. 1932. Cover of a promotional
booklet for the Dutch telephone company

Küpper, Albert Johan Funke (Germany 1894-The
Netherlands 1934) M.A. Jacobson, Haarlem. 117 x 84 cm,
The Netherlands (Forwards – a socialist newspaper –
your beacon)

GRAPHIC

DESIGN

20TH

CENTURY

The Russian Constructivists rejected the idea of unique art works and aimed to erase the separation of art and labor. They aggressively sought a utilitarian design related to industry and propaganda and new art forms to serve the proletariat.

Klutsis, Gustav Gustavovic (Latvia 1895-USSR 1944)
1931, poster, 'The USSR is the Avant Garde of the World
Proletariat.' 144 x 104 cm, USSR

232

Kulagina, Valentina Nikiforovna (1902-1987). 1930.
93.5 x 68 cm, Russia

Koretsky, Victor (Russia 1909-1998) 'Under Lenin's
banner,' 1932. 120 x 84.5 cm, USSR

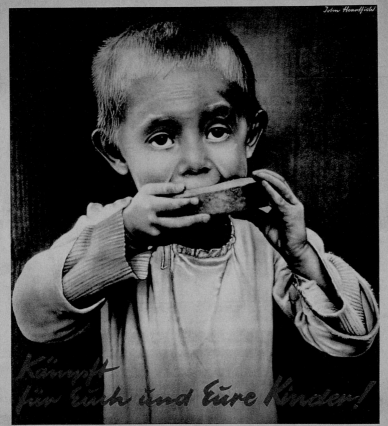

Heartfield, John (pseudonym for Helmut Herzfeld)
(Germany, Berlin 1891-East Berlin 1968) photolitho by
S. Maltz, Berlin, election poster 1932. 72 x 97 cm

160 MILLIONEN IM OSTEN
schreiten froh in die Zukunft!

**Und Du, werktätiges Deutschland!
Erkenne das Zeichen Deiner Kraft!
KÄMPFE
mit der Kommunistischen Partei!
WÄHLE LISTE 3**

Heartfield

Heartfield, John (pseudonym for Helmut Herzfeld)
(Germany, Berlin 1891-East Berlin 1968) 1932, Uranus-
Druckerei GmbH., Berlin. Verantwortlich: Ernst Schneller,
M. d. R., Berlin 1932. 100.5 x 70.5 cm, Germany

Hemberger, Andreas K. (Austria) 1933, Kunst im
Druck GmbH. Munich. 102.5 x 74.5 cm, Germany

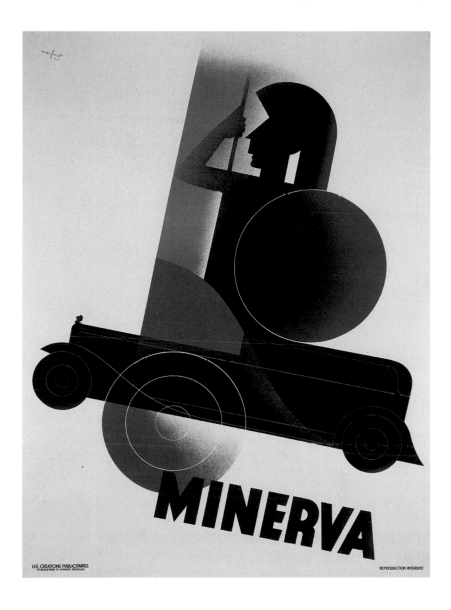

Marfurt, Léo (Switzerland 1894-Belgium 1977) 1931,
Les Créations Publicitaires, Brussels. 160.5 x 119 cm,
Belgium

Leading designers in Czechoslovakia were Ladislav Sutnar and the radical Constructivist Karel Teige, both using photomontage in an incisive manner. Sutnar supported the Constructivist objective to have design standards apply to all aspects of modern life.

G. B. Shaw:

milionářka

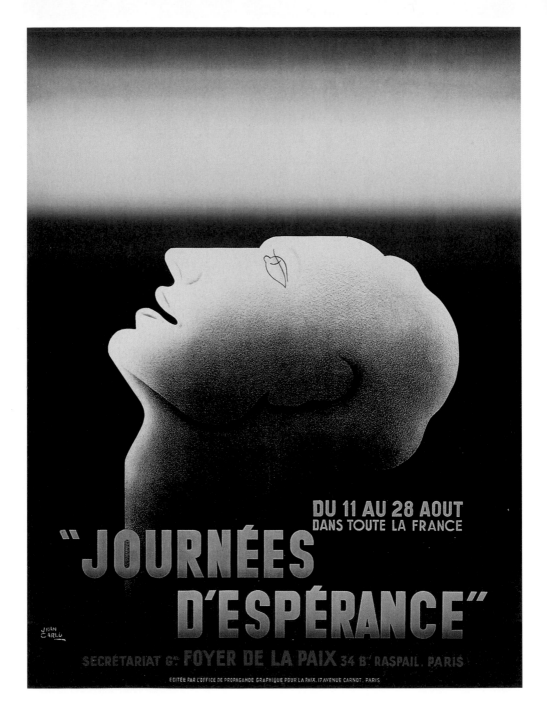

Carlu, Jean George Leon (France, Bonnières-sur-Seine 1900-Paris 1997) 1932. Editée par l'office de la propagande graphique pour la paix, Paris. 156.5 x 117 cm, France

Koelikker, Hermann Alfred (Switzerland 1894-1965)
1932, J.C. Müller, Zürich, 127,5 x 90 cm, Switzerland

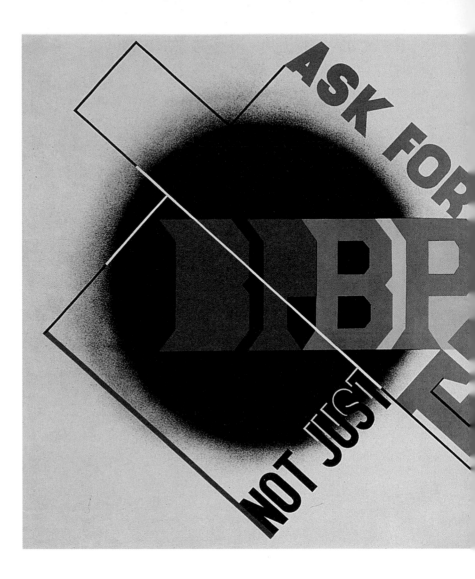

Kauffer, Edward McKnight (USA, Great Falls 1890-
New York City 1954) 1933. 74.5 x 112 cm, United
Kingdom

370 L

Kauffer, Edward McKnight (USA, Great Falls 1890-
New York City 1954) 1930, Vincent Brooks, Day & Son,
Ltd. Lith. London. 101 x 63 cm, United Kingdom

246

Hooykaas, Jacobus (Koos) (The Netherlands 1903-1969)
1930 Steendruk Flach, Sneek. 114.5 x 82 cm, The Netherlands
(for the opening of a new department store in Rotterdam)

Carlu, Jean George Leon (France, Bonnières-sur-Seine
1900-Paris 1997) 1934, Alliance Graphique, Paris.
95.5 x 63 cm, France

Moholy-Nagy, László (Hungary 1895-1946) and
Hartland, Paul (The Netherlands, Apeldoorn, 1910-
1991 Amsterdam) 1934. Full-page advertisement for
Harris Tweed from the trade magazine International
Textiles, Amsterdam, The Netherlands

Viyella (Regd.)

Viyella knitting yarns exactly match Viyella fabrics
Viyella pour le tricot égale exactement les étoffes Viyella
Viyella breigarens evenaren nauwkeurig Viyella stoffen
Viyella-Strickgarne passen ganz genau zu Viyella-Stoffen

Write for patterns to   Demandez les échantillons de   **WILLIAM HOLLINS & Co. Ltd.**   International Textiles — Studio
Vraagt monsters aan   Verlangen Sie Muster von   16, Viyella House, NOTTINGHAM

Satomi, Munetsugu (Japan 1900-1995) 1933. 99 x 61.5 cm,
The Netherlands

Satomi, Munetsugu (Japan 1900-1995) 1934.
Cote d'Azur. PLM. Satomi Le Novateur, Paris.
99 x 62 cm, France

Bill, Max (Switzerland, Winterthur 1908-Germany, Berlin 1994) c. 1933, Gebr. Fretz A.G., Zürich. 100 x 55.5 cm, Switzerland

Pregartbauer, Lois (Austria 1899-1971) 1934. E. Danzinger, Wien. 95 x 63 cm, Austria

Bernard, Francis (France 1909-1979) c. 1932, Editions
Paul Martial, Paris 1932. 99 x 62 cm, France

DAMASCUS BAGHDAD 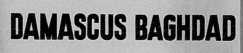 **IN 4 HOURS**

AIR·ORIENT

THE QUICKEST ROUTE OVER THE DESERT

GRAPHIC

DESIGN

20TH

CENTURY

The International Style was the most important Swiss contribution to graphic design following World War II. Reliable and predictable, it was based on logical analysis and an objective presentation of information.

herbert matter

Vacanze invernali – Vacanze ideali

SVIZZERA

Neuburg, Hans (Switzerland 1904-1983) & **Anton
Stankowksi** (photography) 1934, Ringer & Co AG,
Zofingen. 127 x 90 cm, Switzerland

Matter, Herbert (Switzerland, Engelberg 1907-USA,
Springs 1984) 1935. Engelberg, Trübsee, A. Trüb & Cie
Aarau. 102 x 64 cm, Switzerland

Matter, Herbert (Switzerland, Engelberg 1907-USA,
Springs 1984) 1936, Tiefdruck Conzett & Huber, Zürich.
102 x 63.5 cm, Switzerland

Lavies, Jan Frederik (The Netherlands, 1902-
Gorinchem) c. 1936, Offsetdruk J. Smulders & Co.,
The Hague. 118.5 x 88 cm, The Netherlands

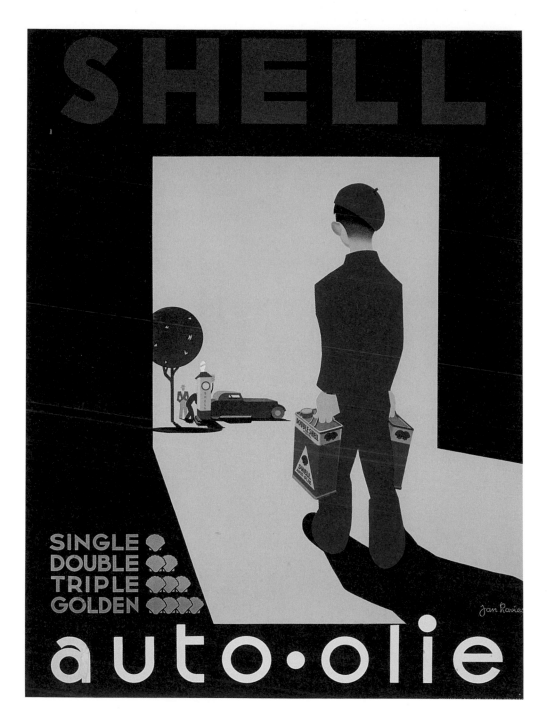

Sandberg, Willem J.H.B. (The Netherlands,
Amersfoort, 1897-Amsterdam, 1984) 1935. Brochure for
an Exhibition on advertising art, Stedelijk Museum,
Amsterdam, The Netherlands

Colin, Paul (France, 1892-1986) 1937 c. 110 x 70 cm,
France

abcdefghijklmnopqrs

tuvwxyz

1234567890

ABCDEFGHIJKLM

NOPQRSTUVWXYZ

.,-:;!?''-(*[—&%

William Addison Dwiggins 1880-1956, USA. Type designer, printer, typographer, graphic designer – studied at the Frank Holme School of Illustration in Chicago under Frederic W. Goudy.

Fonts Metro (1929-30), Electra (1935-49), Caledonia (1938), Eldorado (1953), Falcon (1961) and numerous other designs that were never manufactured.

Electra Venecian Old Face fonts had a strong influence
on typeface design in the 1930s and 1940s in England.
Such influence is evident in the font Electra, designed
by William A. Dwiggins for Linotype in 1935. Electra
combines its classic roots with the zeitgeist of the
1930s, also displaying characteristics of the Bauhaus
and Art Deco styles.

abcdefg

abcdefg

abcdefg

abcdefg

abcdefg

abcdefg

abcdefg

abcdefg

Madrileños!
Cataluña os ama...

Palabras pronunciadas por el Presidente Companys, en el mítin celebrado en la Monumental el 14 de Marzo de 1937, en ocasión del DIA de MADRID.

EDITAT PEL COMISSARIAT DE PROPAGANDA DE LA GENERALITAT DE CATALUNYA.

GRAF. ULTRA S.A. CORCEGA 220. BARCELONA.

Agullo (Spain) 1937, Graf. Ultra S.A. Barcelona.
110 x 76 cm, Spain

Kauffer, Edward McKnight (USA, Great Falls 1890-
New York City 1954) front cover of a catalogue of
posters by the artist, published in 1937 on behalf of the
trustees of the Museum of Modern Art in New York

Moerkerk, Herman (The Netherlands, 's-Hertogenbosch,
1879-Haarlem, 1949) c. 1938. 187 x 123.5 cm, The
Netherlands

unter mitarbeit

gewerbemuseum basel   ausstel

de

Tschichold, Jan (Germany, Leipzig 1902-
Switzerland, Locarno 1974) 1938, Benno Schwabe,
Basel, 63 x 89 cm, Switzerland

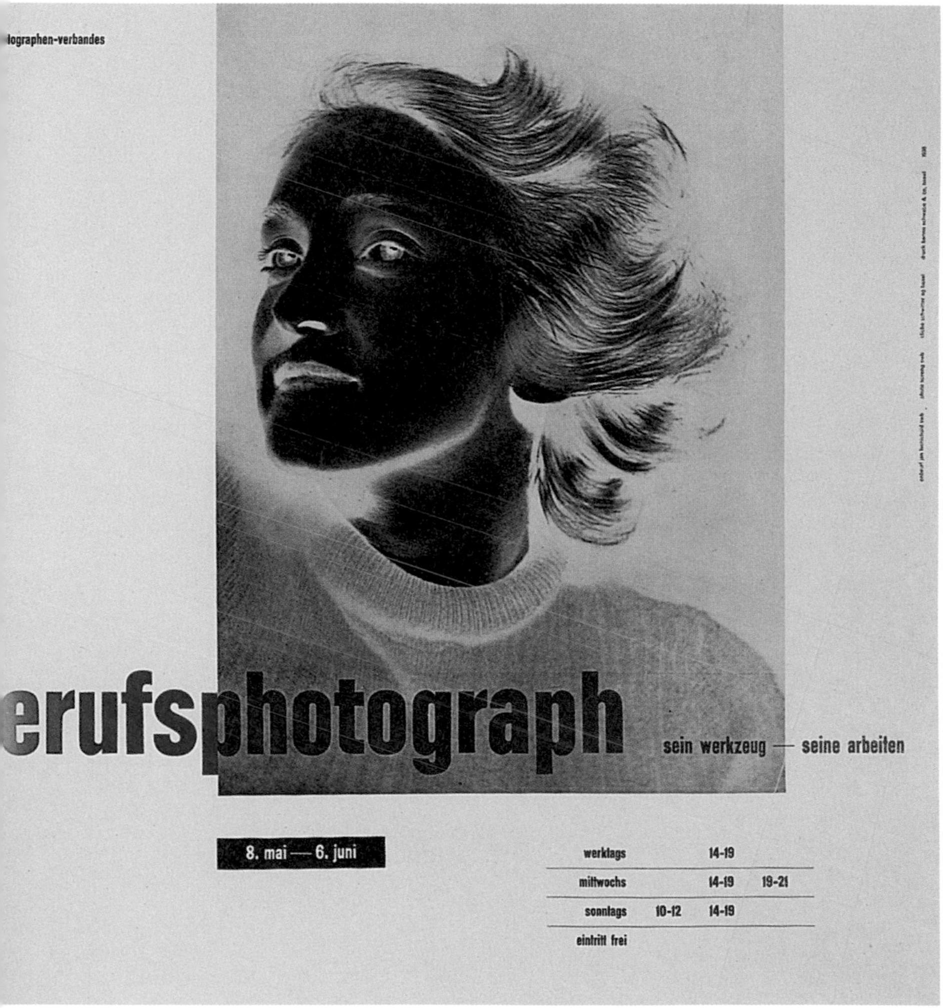
ographen-verbandes
erufsphotograph
sein werkzeug — seine arbeiten
8. mai — 6. juni
werktags 14-19
mittwochs 14-19 19-21
sonntags 10-12 14-19
eintritt frei

U.S.A.: Bevölkerung

1783

1850

1930

Jede Figur 5 Millionen Menschen

Angefertigt für das Bibliographische Institut AG., Leipzig
Gesellschafts- und Wirtschaftsmuseum in Wien

Gesellschaft und Wirtschaft 21

Arntz, Gerd (Germany, Remscheid 1900-The Netherlands, The Hague 1988). 1931. Pictograms for USA: Bevölkerung, from 'Atlas Gesellschaft und Wirtschaft', Institute Leipzig, Germany

Arntz, Gerd (Germany, Remscheid 1900-The
Netherlands, The Hague 1988). 1940. Pictograms
for World Empires, from Otto Neurath, 'De Moderne
Mensch Ontstaat' (Modern Man in Making). Noord-
Hollandsche Uitgevers Maatschappij, Amsterdam,
The Netherlands

Binder, Joseph (Germany 1898-USA 1972) 1939,
N.Y.W.F. Grinnell Litho. Co., Inc., New York.
76 x 50.5 cm, USA

ЗАЩИТА ОТЕЧЕСТВА ЕСТЬ СВЯЩЕННЫЙ

Koretsky, Victor (Russia 1909-1998) 1941.
69.5 x 105.5 cm, USSR

Stoecklin, Niklaus (Switzerland, Basel 1896-Riehen
1982) 1941, Wasserman AG, Basel. 127 x 90 cm,
Switzerland

Huber, Max (Switzerland, Zürich 1919-1992) 1948,
Ind. Graf. N. Moneta, Milan. 139 x 97 cm, Italy

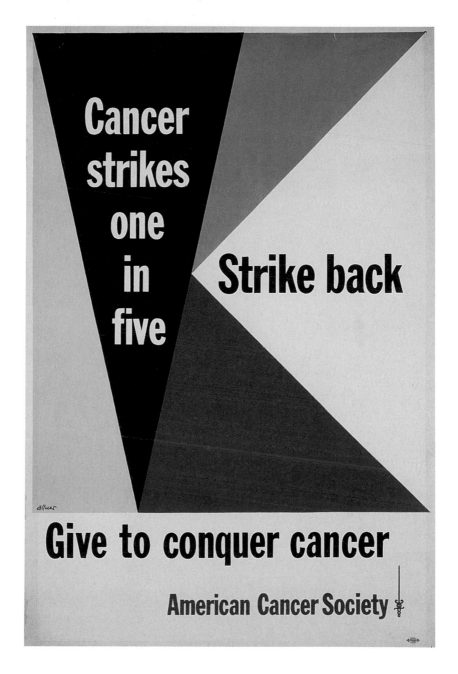

Allner, Walter Heinz (Germany, Dessau 1909-USA)
1952, Amalgamated Lithographers of America,
New York. 115.5 x 76 cm, USA

Matter, Herbert (Switzerland, Engelberg 1907-USA,
Springs 1984) 1950, Litho. in USA. 116 x 73.5 cm, USA

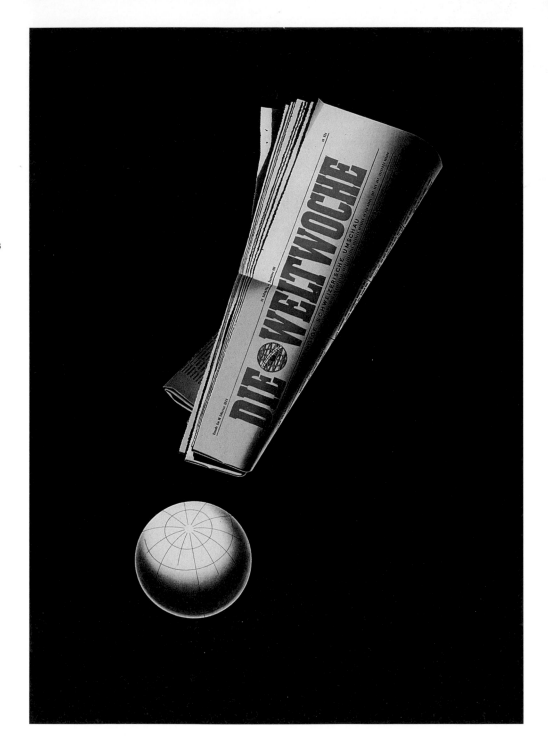

Leupin, Herbert (Switzerland, Beinwill 1916-Basel 1999)
1949, Wolfsberg Druck, Zürich, 128 x 90 cm, Switzerland

Ensem (?) 1950. Bengtson Litografiska AB,
Stockholm, Bonnier. 50 x 35 cm, Sweden

In the United States, the older postwar poster generation included giants such as Paul Rand, Lester Beall, and Saul Bass. Noted for his work as a designer, educator, and writer on design, Rand remained a dominant and inspiring force until his death in 1996.

Is it
a question
...or
an answer

no way out

Darryl F. Zanuck presents **No Way Out**

starring: **Richard Widmark**

Linda Darnell

Stephen McNally

with: Sidney Poitier, Mildred Joanne Smith
Harry Bellaver, Stanley Ridges, Dots Johnson

produced by: **Darryl F. Zanuck**

directed by: **Joseph L. Mankiewicz**

Written by Joseph L. Mankiewicz and Lesser Samuels

20th
CENTURY-FOX

Nitsche, Erik (Switzerland 1908-USA 1998) 1950, 105 x 69 cm, USA

Pintori, Giovanni (Sardinia, Tresnuraghes 1912-Italy 1998) 1949, Officine Grafiche ricordi S.P.A. Milan. 70 x 49.5 cm, Italy

294

Elfer, Arpad Designed & produced by Colman Prentis
and Varley Ltd. c. 1950. 76 x 101 cm, United Kingdom

Lohrer, Hanns (Germany 1912-) 1955. Imp. en
Allemagne. Printed in Germany. 59 x 41.5 cm, Germany

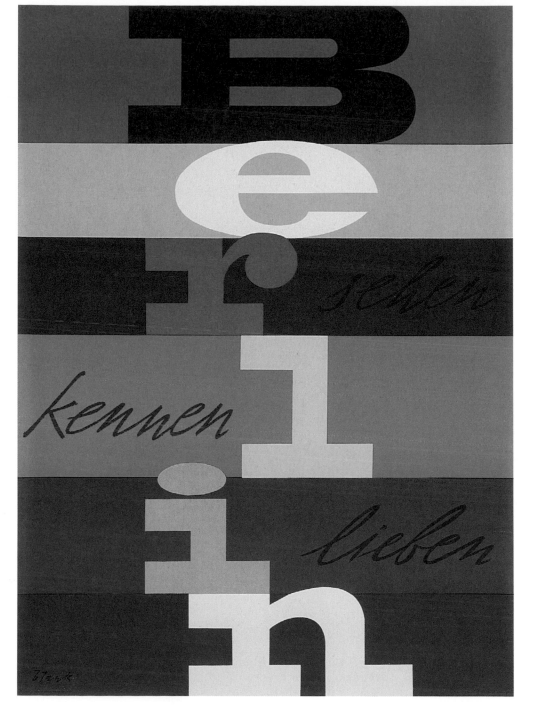

Blank, Richard (Germany 1901-1972) c. 1955, August
Raabe, Berlin-Neukölln. 84 x 60 cm, Germany

Müller-Brockmann, Josef Mario (Switzerland,
Rapperswil 1914-Unterengstringen 1996) 1952/53,
A. Trüb & Cie. 128 x 90 cm, Switzerland

Stankowsky, Anton (Germany, Gelsenkirchen 1906-
Stuttgart 1998) c. 1951. 84.5 x 59 cm, Germany

Funk 1952. Die neue Ausstellung der graphischen
Abteilung der Staatl. Akademie der Bild. Künste,
Stuttgart. 84.5 x 60 cm, Germany

Fischer, Heini (Switzerland, Egerkingen 1921-) 1952,
city-druck ag, Zürich. 128 x 90.5 cm, Switzerland

304

Munsong, Stefan P. (Germany) Photos: Amann 1951,
Seelig & co. 83.5 x 59 cm, Germany

Aicher, Ofl (Germany 1922-1991) Hochschule für
Gestaltung Ulm 1954, 59 × 41.5 cm, Germany

306

Roth, Dieter (Germany, Hannover 1930) 1954. Drupa.
druck: Wilhelm Greve, Berlin. Herausgeber: NOWEA,
Düsseldorf. 84 x 59.5 cm, Germany

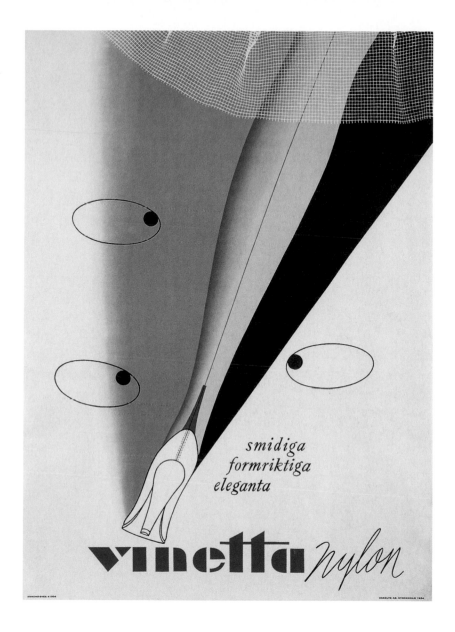

smidiga
formriktiga
eleganta

vinetta *nylon*

NN 1954, Annons-Svea. Esselte AB, Stockholm.
70 x 50 cm, Sweden

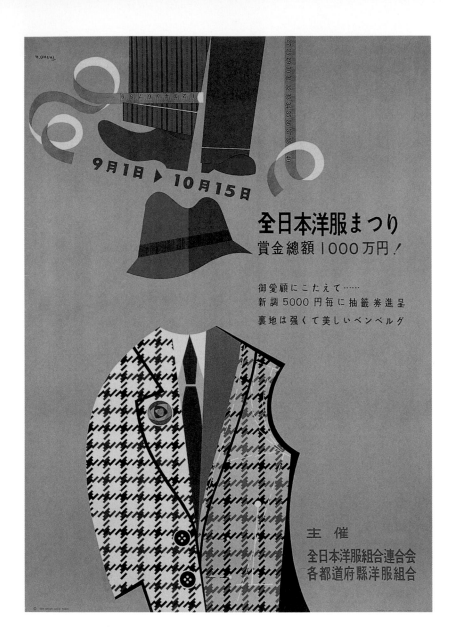

Ohchi, Hiroshi (Japan, Tokyo 1908-Tokyo 1974) Japan,
c. 1954

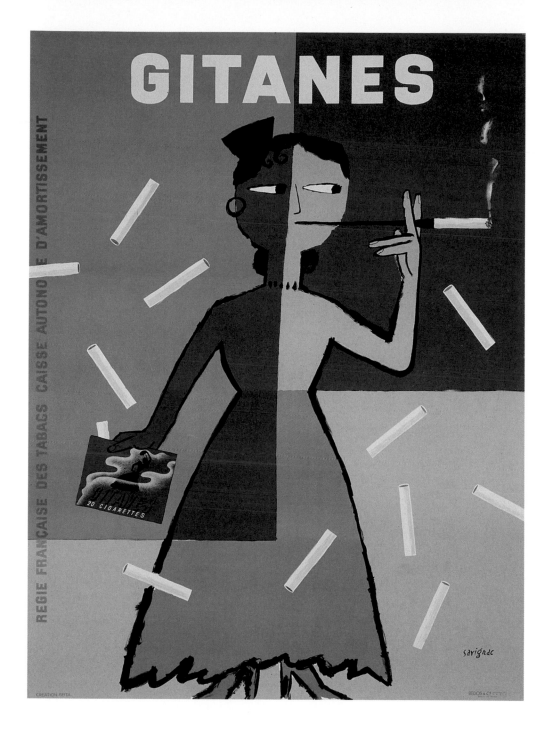

Savignac, Raymond (France, Paris 1907-) 1954, Bedos
& Cie, Paris Creation Seita. 161.5 x 121 cm, France

abcdefghijklmno

pqrstuvwxyz

1234567890

ABCDEFGHIJKLMN

OPQRSTUVWXYZ

.,-:;!?''-(*[&%—

Adrian Frutiger. 1928 Switzerland. Contemporary Swiss graphic designer, typographer, and type designer of imagination and consummate craftsmanship, associated with **Deberny & Peignot**, **Bauer** and **Linotype**.

Fonts Apollo, Avenir, Frutiger, Meridien, OCR-B, Univers, etc.

Univers The Univers family of fonts designed by Adrian Frutiger more than forty years ago is one of the most innovative type creations of the modern age. Its introduction prompted a reappraisal of the sans serif.

While the forms of the Univers have their roots in the old grotesque types, they also combine features that rebel against the past. They carry in them the knowledge that type is part of the cultural heritage handed down from our forefathers, a heritage that we should neither ignore or alter and that we should pass on to future generations.

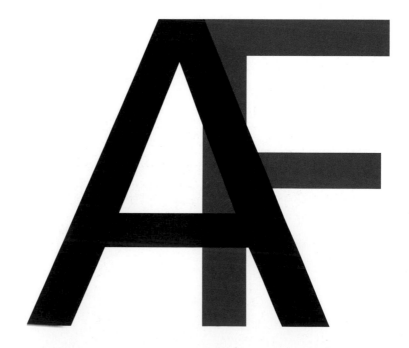

314

Mettes, Franciscus Joseph Engbertus (Frans)
(The Netherlands, Amsterdam 1909-1984) ZAP, c. 1950,
photolitho, 116 x 83 cm

Lillmor, Lars (Sweden) 1955. Svenska Tryckeri.
99.5 x 70 cm, Sweden

Leupin, Herbert (Switzerland, Beinwill 1916-Basel 1999)
1955. Paul Bender, Zollikon-Zürich. 126.5 x 90 cm,
Switzerland

Leupin, Herbert (Switzerland, Beinwill 1916-Basel 1999)
1955. Imprimeries Réunies S.A., Lausanne Dpt. Offset.
128 x 90 cm, Switzerland

Ito, Kenji c. 1955. 101 x 72.5 cm, Japan

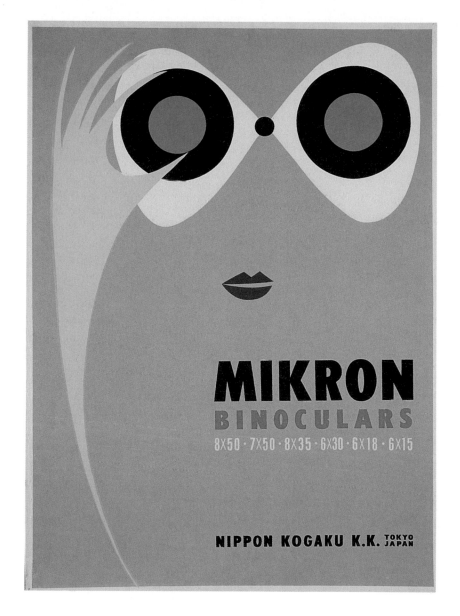

Kamekura, Yusaku (Japan, Yoshida 1915-Tokyo 1997)
c. 1955, Nippon Kogaku K K Tokyo Japan. 105.5 x 76 cm,
Japan

Ohchi, Hiroshi (Japan, Tokyo 1908-Tokyo 1974)
c. 1955. 101.5 x 72.5 cm, Japan

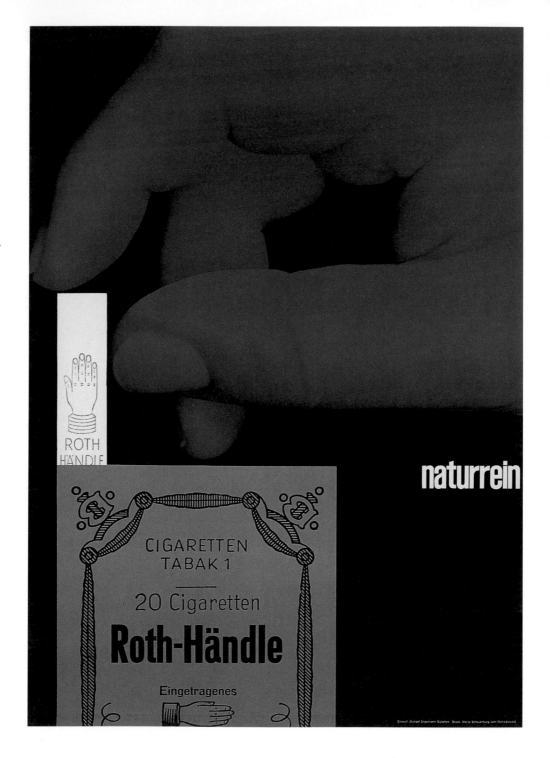

Engelmann, Michael (Czechoslovakia, Prague 1928-
Germany, München) 1955. Moritz Schauenburg
Lahr/Schwarzwald. 118.5 x 83.5 cm, Germany

Engelmann, Michael (Czechoslovakia, Prague
1928-Germany, Munich) 1955, Moritz Schauenburg
Lahr/Schwarzwald. 118.5 x 82.5 cm, Germany

Swierzy, Waldemar (Poland, Katowice 1931- Warsaw)
1956. Otello. 84.5 x 58 cm, Poland

GRAPHIC

DESIGN

20TH

CENTURY

Polish designers developed a strong national style during the 1950s and 1960s. Their designs, especially posters, incorporated painted illustrations, photography, and hand lettering and were infused with symbolism, metaphors, and a unique adaptation of surrealism.

Rio Escondido

Film produkcji meksykańskiej

Scenariusz i reżyseria: Emilio Fernandez

Zdjęcia: Gabriel Figueroa

Produkcja: Reul de Anda

Wykonawcy:
Maria Felix
Carlus Lapez Moctepuma
Fernando Fernandez
i in.

Gabor 1956. Athenaeum. 83 x 57 cm, Poland

Brunck, Gert 1957 Graphische Werke Germania.
Druckerei KG, Kiel. 83.5 x 59.5 cm, Germany

Lipinski, Eryk (Poland, 1908-1991) 1957. Nowa Gwinea.
CWF. 84 x 58 cm, Poland

Sandberg, Willem J.H.B. (The Netherlands,
Amersfoort 1897-Amsterdam 1984) 1957. Cover of
the Stedelijk Museum's library catalogue, Amsterdam,
The Netherlands

Vertical text in the poster design:
BECH
ELECTRONIC
CENTRE

Gerstner, Karl (Switzerland, Basel 1930-) and
Kutter, Markus (Switzerland, Beggingen 1925-) 1959,
90 x 128 cm, printed by Wasserman AG, Basel

NN Austria, 1959

Roligkawnej, W. 84.5 x 58.5 cm, Poland

NN Poland, c. 1960

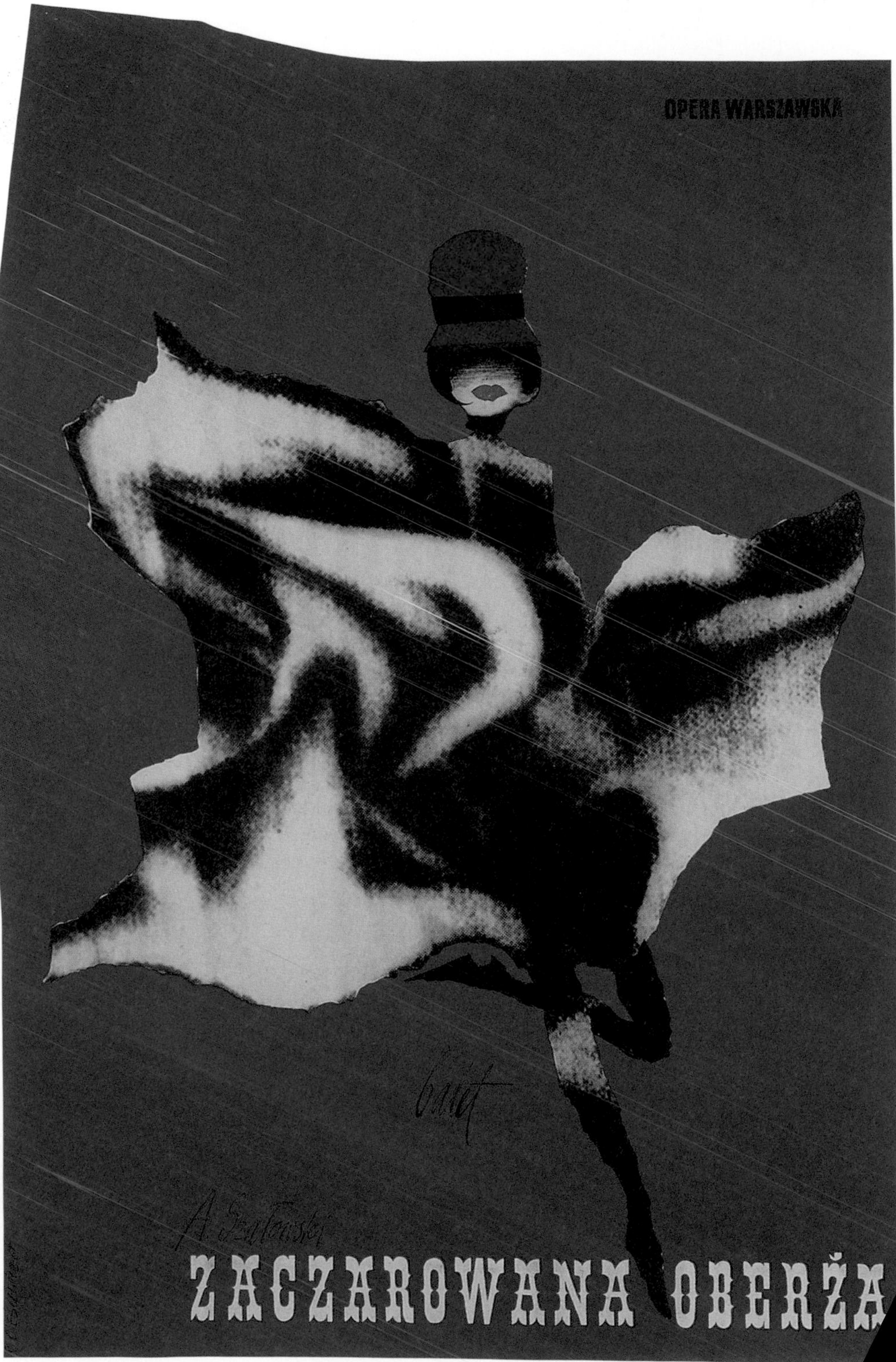
OPERA WARSZAWSKA
balet
ZACZAROWANA OBERŻA

… i głowa spokojna

Ubezpieczenia przyjmują inspektoraty PZU i ajenci ubezpieczeniowi

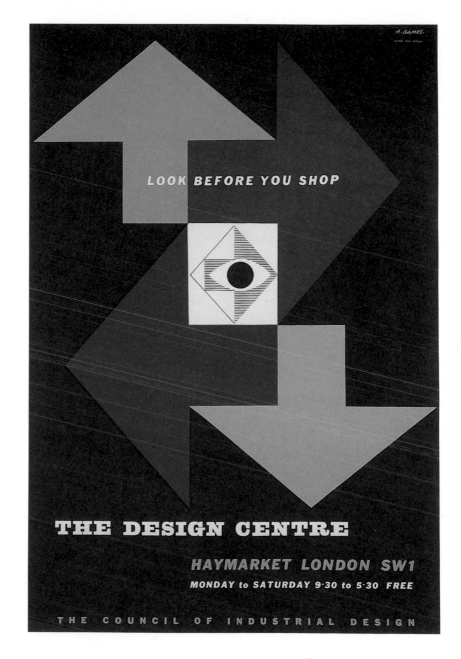

Games, Abram (United Kingdom, London 1914-1996)
c. 1960, United Kingdom

Games, Abram (United Kingdom, London 1914-1996)
c. 1960, Mills & Rockleys (production) Ltd, Ipswich.
50.5 x 76 cm, United Kingdom

343

Engelmann, Pavel Michael (Czechoslovakia, Prague
1928-Germany, 1966) 1955, Moritz Schauenburg
Lahr/Schwarzwald. 118.5 x 83.5 cm, Germany

Entwurf: Michael Engelmann München Druck: Moritz Schauenburg Lahr/Schwarzwald

Fangor, Wojciech (Poland 1922-) 1959. CWF. 83.5 x 58 cm,
Poland

Swierzy, Waldemar (Poland, Katowice 1931- Warsaw)
1959. CWF. 84.5 x 58.5 cm, Poland

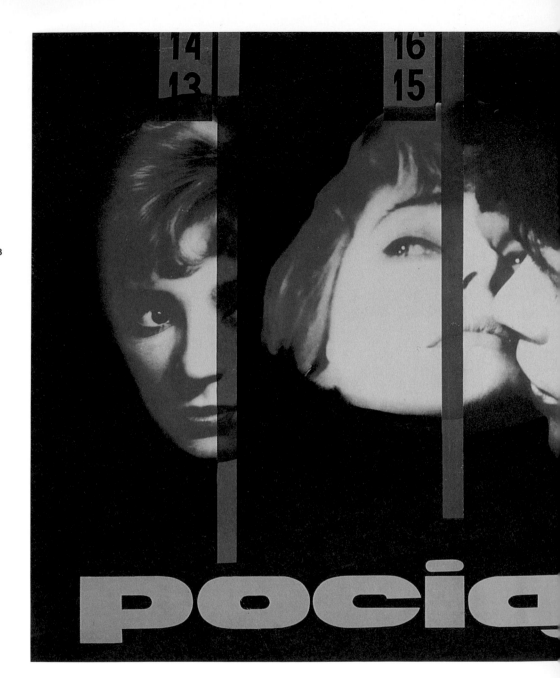

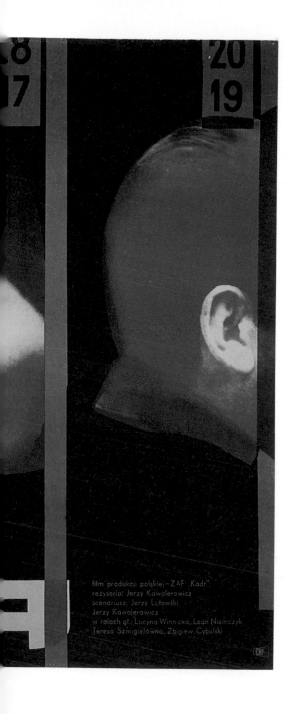

Zamecznik, Wojciech (Poland, Warsaw 1923-)
1959 (Der Zug). 97.5 x 130 cm, Poland

meubels A P originals

furniture meubles möbel mobili

Wernars, Gerard (The Netherlands, Amsterdam
1924-) 1959, Steendrukkerij de Jong & Co, Hilversum.
95 x 69 cm, The Netherlands

Herman
Miller
Collection

Verkauf ab
9. März
Contura SA
Basel
Aeschen
vorstadt 4
Passage

Möbel unserer Zeit

Hofmann, Armin (Switzerland, Winterthur 1920-)
1962, Wasserman AG. 127.5 x 90 cm, Switzerland

abcdefghijklmnopq

rstuvwxyz

1234567890

ABCDEFGHIJKLMN

OPQRSTUVWXYZ

.,-:;!?''-(*[&%—

Hermann Zapf 1918 Germany. Book designer, creator of textfaces for books, magazines, and newspapers.

Fonts Arabic, Cyrillic, Greek, Scripts, Zapfino, the Zapf Dingbats, Palatino, Optima, Melior.

Optima Optima, designed by Hermann Zapf, combines

the clarity of Modern Face with the objectivity of sans-

serif typefaces. He was influenced by the stone inlay

alphabets of Roman antiquity as well as typefaces of

the early Renaissance. The clear, elegant characters

of Optima can often be seen in advertisements,

especially for cosmetics.

ABCDEabcde

ABCDEabcde

ABCDEabcde

ABCDEabcde

ABCDEabcde

ABCDEabcde

ABCDEabcde

ABCDEabcde

fg

Zéro (Schleger, Hans) (Kempen, Prussia 1898-United Kingdom, London 1976) 1958. 76 x 50.5 cm, United Kingdom

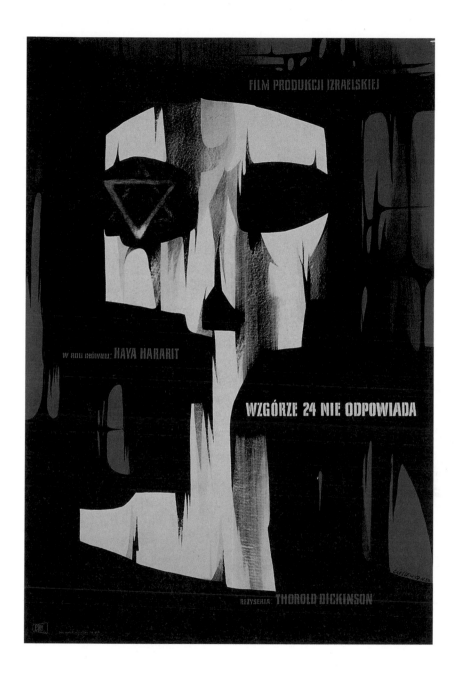

NN Poland, c. 1960

358

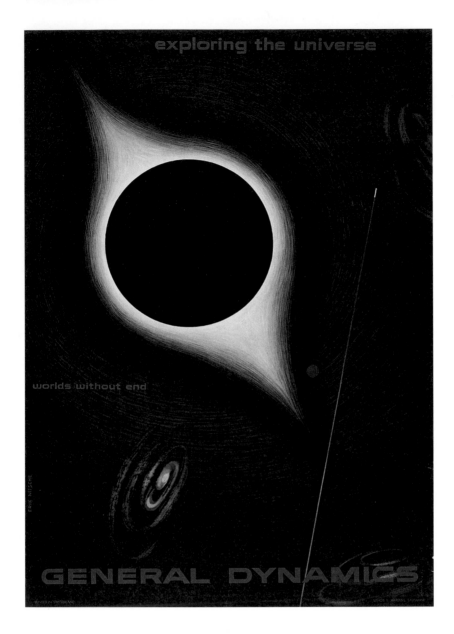

Nitsche, Erik (Switzerland, Lausanne 1908-USA 1998)
1958, Lithos R. Massens, Lausanne. 120.5 x 86 cm,
Switzerland

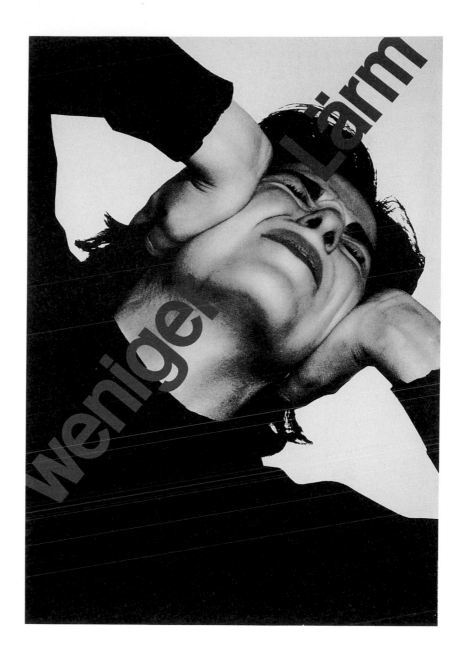

Müller-Brockmann, Josef Mario (Switzerland,
Rapperswil 1914-Unterengstringen 1996) 1960, Lith.
u. Cartonage AG, Zürich. 128 x 90 cm, Switzerland

360

Mitzkat, P. 1960. Wassermann AG. 128 x 90 cm,
Switzerland

kunstgewerbemuseum zürich

dokumentation über marcel duchamp

30. juni—28. august 1960 . sa/so: 10—12 + 14—17 . mo: 14—18 . di—fr: 10—12 + 14—18 + 20—22

Bill, Max (Switzerland, Winterthur 1908-Germany, Berlin 1994) 1960. Bollman-druck. Kunstgewerbe-museum, Zürich. 128 x 90 cm, Switzerland

abcdefghijklmnopqr

stuvwxyz

1234567890

ABCDEFGHIJKLMN

OPQRSTUVWXYZ

.,-:;!?''-(*[&%—

Adrian Frutiger 1928 Switzerland. Contemporary Swiss graphic designer, typographer, and type designer of imagination and consummate craftsmanship, associated with **Deberny & Peignot**, **Bauer**, and **Linotype**.

Fonts Apollo, Avenir, Frutiger, Meridien, OCR-B, Univers, etc.

Apollo The text typeface Apollo was designed by Adrian Frutiger in 1962 and produced by Monotype. It is oddly one of the lesser known typefaces of Frutiger, perhaps due to the extreme fame of some of his other fonts, like the typefaces Frutiger and Univers. Stylistically, the very legible and harmonic Apollo font is an old face. Frutiger designed it especially for the photosetting used at the time.

The Apollo font family consists of the weights roman and semibold and their respective italics as well as expert sets. Frutiger optimized the relation between the two weights so that the roman is robust enough to present a legible text on soft paper but light enough to contrast with the semibold. The clear, elegant Apollo font is perfect for headlines as well as long texts. Apollo is a trademark of Monotype Typography.

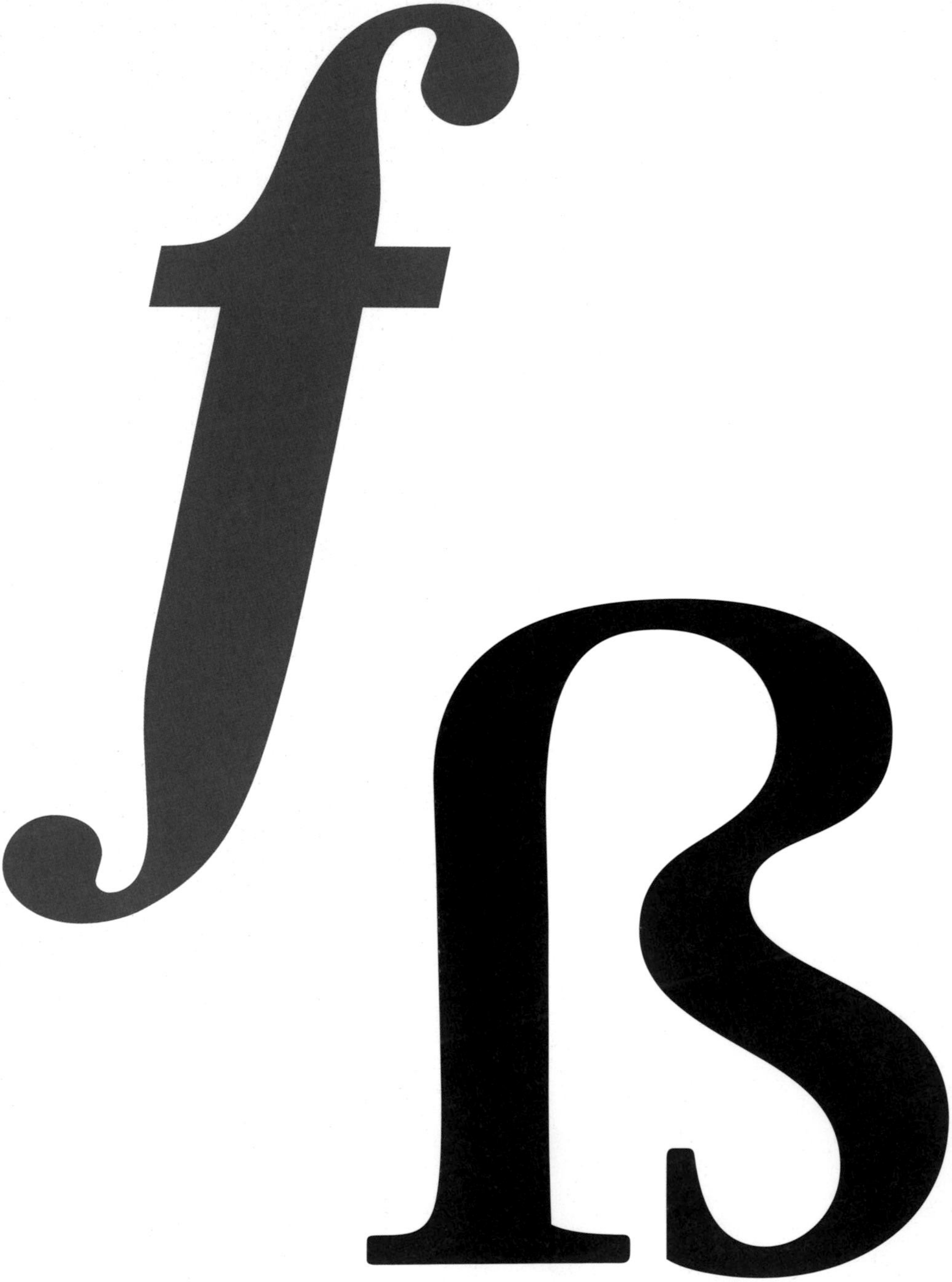

¶

Pintori, Giovanni (Sardinia, Tresnuraghes 1912-Italy
1998) 1962. Graf. N. Monata S.P.A. Milano. 70 x 50 cm,
Italy.

Zagorski, S. 1962. WAG. 97.5 x 67.5 cm, Poland

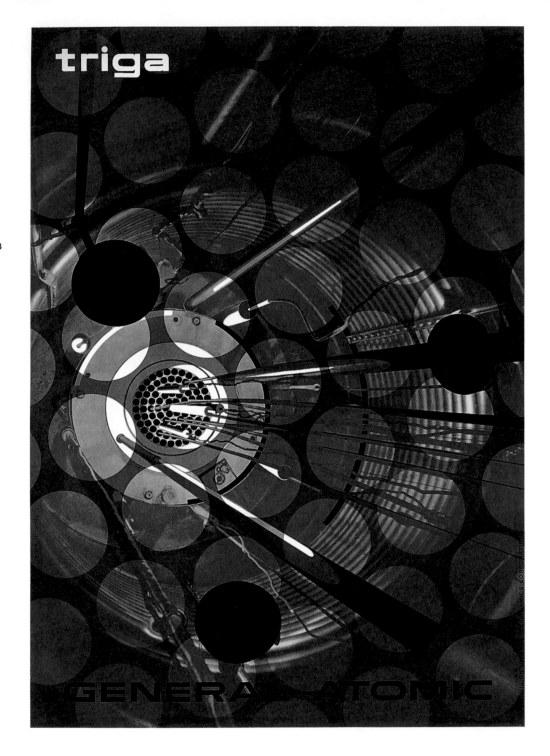

triga

GENERAL ATOMIC

Nitsche, Erik (Switzerland, Lausanne 1908-USA,
Ridgefield 1998) 1962. 127 x 89 cm, USA

F.K. 1962. Mokép film. 81.5 x 56 cm, Hungary

Michel, Hans (Germany, Weimar 1920-1996) and
Kieser, Günther (Germany, Kronberg im Taunus 1930-)
1962, novum. 85 x 118.5 cm, Germany

Elffers, Dick (The Netherlands 1910-1990), 1960,
De Jong & Co, Hilversum. 100 x 62 cm, The Netherlands

Kamekura, Yusaku (Japan, 1915-1997) 1962.
Dai Nippon Printing Co. 104 x 72.5 cm, Japan

Starowieyski, Franciszek (Poland 1930-) 1960. CWF.
58 x 84.5 cm, Poland

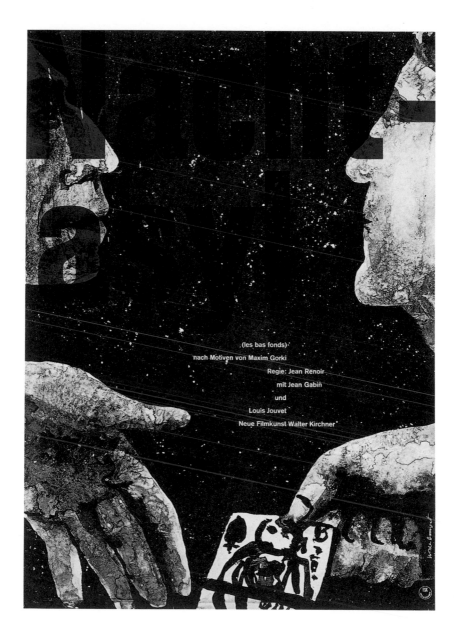

Baumgart, Isolde (Germany) 1960. FSK. 83 x 59 cm,
Germany

Matter, Herbert (Switzerland, Engelberg 1907-USA,
Springs 1984) c. 1960. 128 x 90 cm, printed by
Wasserman AG, Basel

GIACOMETTI

KUNSTHALLE BASEL   25. JUNI - 28. AUGUST

Henrion, Frederick Henri Kay (Germany, Nürnberg
1914-United Kingdom, London 1990) 1960. 75.5 x 50 cm,
United Kingdom

Wirth, Kurt (Switzerland, Bern 1917) c. 1960. Photo:
Winkler, Albert Gebr. Fretz AG. 127.5 x 90 cm,
Switzerland

Rüegg, Ruedi (Switzerland, Zurich 1936-) 1960.
Gebr. Fretz AG, Zürich. 127 x 90.5 cm, Switzerland

Looser, Hans (Switzerland 1919-1988) 1960.
Photochromdruck Paul Bender, Zollikon-Zürich.
128 x 90 cm, Switzerland

Tilley, Patrick (Great Britain) 1960. 75.5 x 50 cm,
United Kingdom

Tilley, Patrick (Great Britain) 1960. 75.5 x 50 cm, United Kingdom

Tilley, Patrick (Great Britain) 1960. 75.5 x 50 cm, United Kingdom

Mavignier, Almir da Silva (Brazil, Rio de Janeiro
1925-) 1960, Siebdruck Miller Museum Ulm.
84 x 59 cm, Germany

arp

museum ulm
täglich
10 - 12 + 14 - 17 uhr
außer montag
vom 20. 9.
bis 16. 10.
1960

skulpturen
reliefs
teppiche
gouachen
zeichnungen
grafik

Monnerat, Pierre (France, Paris 1907-Switzerland,
Lausanne) 1961. Roth + Sauter SA, Lausanne.
125 x 90 cm, Switzerland

Hofmann, Armin (Switzerland, Winterthur 1920-)
1963. 128 x 90.5 cm, Switzerland

392

Bruna, Dick (The Netherlands, Utrecht 1927) 1963.
Offsetdruk Steendrukkerij de Jong & Co., Hilversum.
116 x 82.5 cm, The Netherlands

393

Bruna, Dick (The Netherlands, Utrecht 1927) 1967.
Offsetdruk Steendrukkerij de Jong & Co., Hilversum.
116 x 82.5 cm, The Netherlands

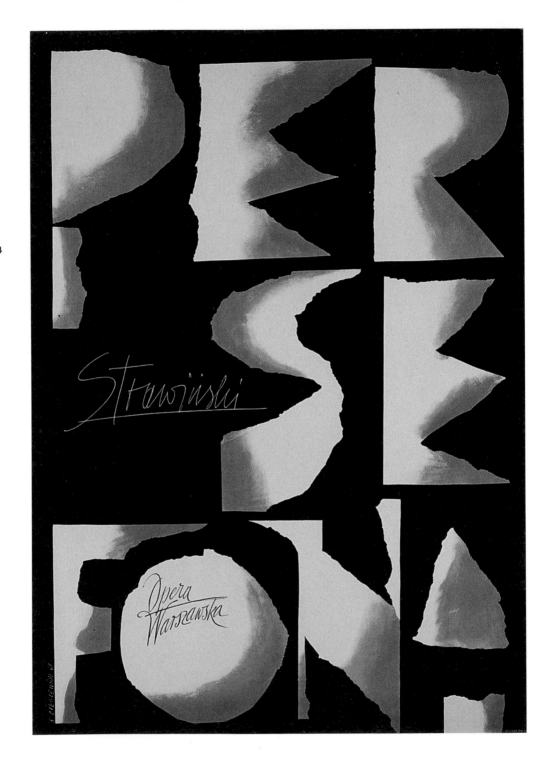

Cieslewicz, Roman (Poland, Lwow 1930-France 1996)
1961. 95 x 67 cm, Poland

Cieslewicz, Roman (Poland, Lwow 1930-France 1996)
1961. 63 x 48 cm, Poland

Fangor, Wojciech (Poland 1922-) c. 1961. 84 x 59 cm,
Poland

TK (?) (Germany) 1961. 85 x 59.5 cm, Germany

Lipinski, Eryk (Poland, 1908-1991) 1961, 83.5 x 58.5 cm,
Poland

Lohrer, Hanns (Germany, Stuttgart 1912) 1962. Repro.
u. D.: Autenrieth, Stuttgart. 119 x 84 cm, Germany

Piatti, Celestino (Switzerland, Wangen 1922-) Photo:
Siegfried, 1962, VSK, Basel. 127.5 x 90 cm, Switzerland

Lipinski, Eryk (Poland, 1908-1991) Bialowlosa 1962.
Opera Warszawska. 98.5 x 67.5 cm, Poland

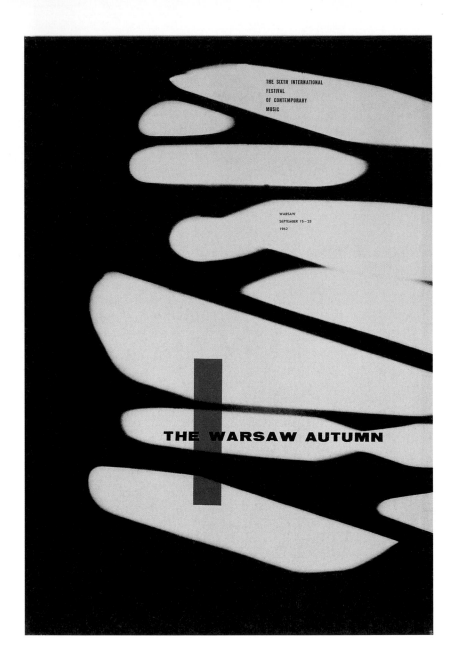

Zamecnik, Wojzeck (Poland, Warsaw 1923-) 1962.
97.5 x 67 cm, Poland

Hillmann (novum), Hans (Germany, Niedermois 1925-
Kassel) 1965. repro. & D: P.R. Wilk, F/m. Neue filmkunst
Walter Kirchner. 84 x 59 cm, Germany

Swierzy, Waldemar (Poland, Katowice 1931- Warsaw)
1965, 84 x 58.5 cm, Poland

abcdefghijklmnopqrstuvwxyz

1234567890

A B C D E F G H I J

K L M N O P Q R S T

U V W X Y Z

.,-.;.!?"-(*[&%—

Matthew Carter 1937 England. Type designer.

Fonts Snell Roundhand (1966), Cascade Script (1966), Gando Ronde (with H.J. Hunziker, 1966), Olympian (1970), Auriga (1970), Shelley Script (1972), CRT Gothic (1974), Video (1977), Bell Centennial (1978), Galliard (1978), New Baskerville (with John Quaranda, 1978), V&A Titling (1981), Bitstream Charter (1987), Charter (1993), as well as various Greek, Korean, Hebrew, and Indian (Devanagari) typefaces.

Shelly Script Is based on intricate English scripts
of the eighteenth and nineteenth centuries. The musi-
cal terms Andante, Allegro, and Volante were chosen
by Carter to describe the mood of the three different
cuts of his font. Andante is the most reserved, Allegro
has a few more flourishes, and Volante's capital letters
are surrounded with swirling strokes. Perfect for invi-
tations or other cards, Shelley Script, like other fonts
of its kind, seems to appeal particularly to America.

Ñ Œ Õ Ç Ÿ

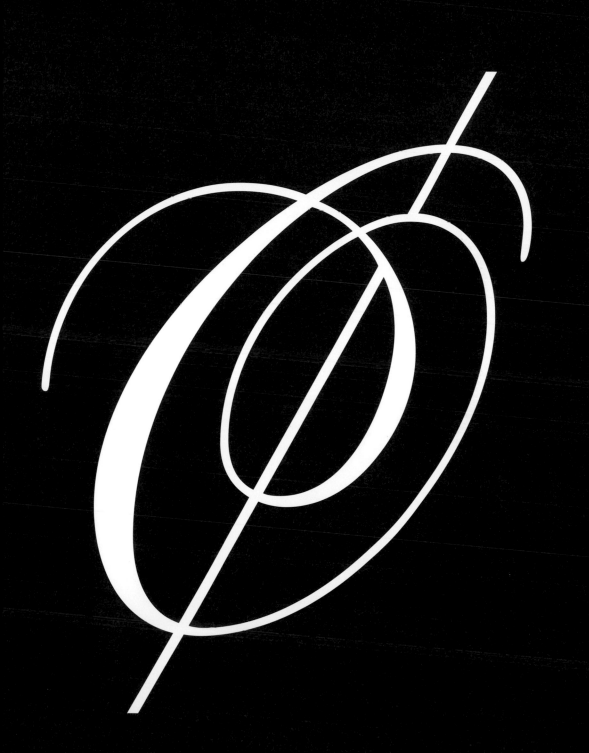

In the United States during the 1960s, designers such as Milton Glaser, a founding member of Push Pin Studio, and Peter Max were among the most popular. Their design approach, at times celebrating the anti-establishment sub-culture, was later broadly labeled by the media as "psychedelic."

413

Wilson, Wes (USA, San Francisco 1936-) 1966. Grateful
Dead. Junior Wells Chicago Blues Band and The Doors.
55.5 x 35.5 cm, USA

415

Wilson, Wes (USA, San Francisco 1936-) and **Robert Wesley** (USA, San Francisco 1936). 1967. Jefferson Airplane. West Coast Lithograph Co., San Fransisco. 59 x 34.5 cm, USA

Schnepf, Bob Family Dog Productions 1967. Photo:
Weir, Thomas. 71 x 27.5 cm, USA

418

Moscoso, Victor (Spain, 1936-) 1967. Neon Rose. The
Miller Blues Band. 56 x 35.5 cm, USA

Martinez, Sue 1967. Matteus Katz Productions.
45.5 x 35.5 cm, USA

English, Michael (United Kingdom 1939–) and **Nigel Weymouth** (United Kingdom) c. 1967. 75.5 x 50 cm, United Kingdom

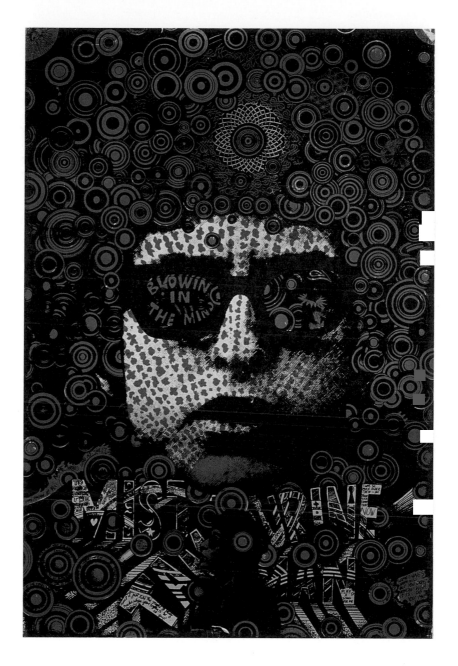

Sharp, Martin (United Kingdom 1942-) c. 1967.
76 x 51 cm, United Kingdom

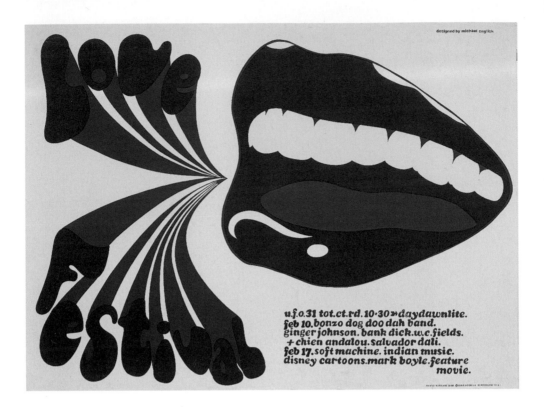

English, Michael (United Kingdom 1939-), 1967
silkscreen

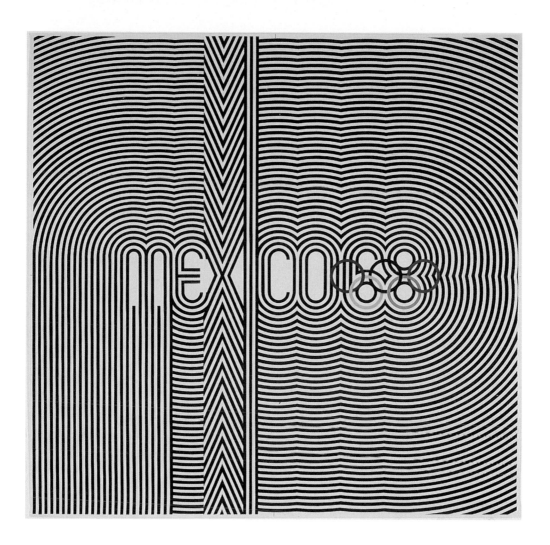

Vasquez, Pedro Ramirez; Terrazas, Eduardo and
Wyman, Lance 1967, Impreso en Mexico por impresos
automaticos de Mexico S.A. 90 x 90 cm, Mexico

Luis Bunuel (Ensayo de un Crimen)   Das   verbrecherische

Leben   des   Archibaldo

de la Cruz   eine makabre Mörderkomödie

Neue Filmkunst Walter Kirchner   aus Mexiko

Hillmann (novum), Hans (Germany, Niedermois
1925-Kassel) 1967. Repro. & D: P.R. Wilk, Frankfurt am
Main. Neue filmkunst Walter Kirchner. 84 x 59 cm,
Germany

426

English, Michael (United Kingdom, 1939-) and
Weymouth, Nigel (United Kingdom) c. 1968. Osiris
Vision Ltd., Westbourne. 74.5 x 49.5 cm, United
Kingdom

Bemting, R. 1968. (?) Cuba. OSPAAL. 54 x 34.5 cm,
Cuba

fifty advertisements of the year
an exhibition in association with
the American Institute of Graphic Arts
at the London School of Printing and Graphic Arts
Back Hill Clerkenwell ec1 15 June - 5 July 10am - 5pm

NN C. 1970, United Kingdom

Crouwel, Wim (The Netherlands, Groningen, 1928)
1966. Exhibition poster Colour Forms, Stedelijk Museum,
Amsterdam, The Netherlands

kleursystematiek
hard edge
colorfieldpainting
minimal art

vormen van de kleur

schilderijen en plastieken uit

engeland
duitsland
frankrijk
nederland
usa
zwitserland

amsterdam
stedelijk museum   19 november 1966 t m 15 januari 1967

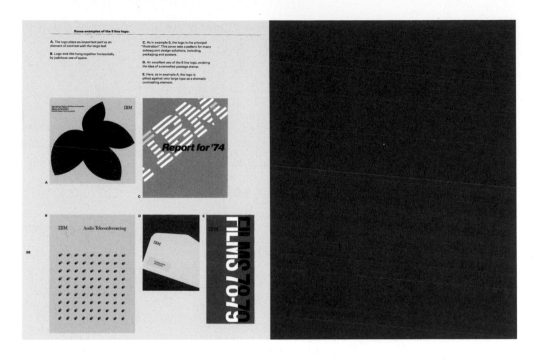

Rand, Paul (USA, New York City 1914-USA 1996).
The IBM Logo. Its use in company identification,
brochure, c. 1970.

abcdefghijklmnop

qrstuvwxyz

1234567890

ABCDEFGHIJKL

MNOPQRSTUVW

XYZ

.,-:;!?""-(*[—&%

Jan Tschichold. 1902–1974, Germany. Typographer, calligrapher, author, teacher.

Fonts Transit (1931), Saskia (1931), Zeus (1931), Sabon (1967).

Sabon In the early sixties, the German masterprinters' association requested that a new typeface be designed and produced in identical form on both Linotype and Monotype machines so that text and technical composition would match. **Walter Cunz** at the **Stempel** responded by commissioning **Jan Tschichold** to design the most faithful version of **Claude Garamond's** serene and classical roman yet to be cut. The boldface and particularly the italic are limited by the twin requirements of Linotype and Monotype hot metal machines. The **Bitstream's** cursive is a return to the form of one of Garamond's late italics, recently identified. Punches and matrices for the romans survive at the Plantin-Moretus Museum, Antwerp.

The name refers to **Jacques Sabon**, who introduced Garamond's romans to Frankfurt, although the typefaces that Sabon himself cut towards the end of the sixteenth century have a faintly awkward style of their own.

433

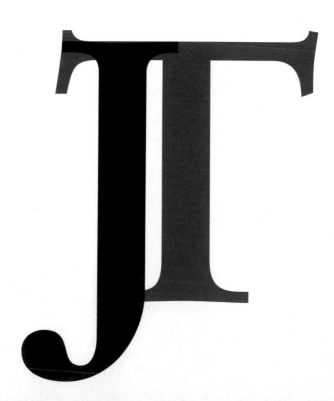

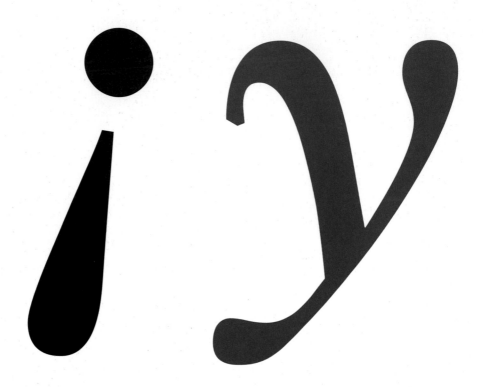

1234567890

1234567890

A MIDSUMMER NIGHT'S DREAM
STAR SPANGLED CREATION SEEMS TO BE REAL
EXPLODES IN A MYTH OF RELENTLESS APPEAL

NN 1970. Midsummer nights dream. 76 x 51.5 cm,
Cuba

438

Dea Trier Morch (Denmark) 1969, linocut.
84.5 x 60 cm, Denmark

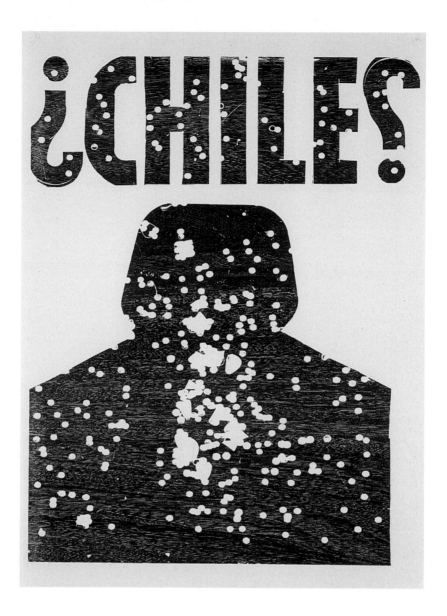

Grieshaber, Helmut Andreas Peter (Germany, Rot
1909-1981) 1973, woodcut by the artist. 77 x 56 cm,
Germany

440

Student workshop, c. 1970. (Berkeley) 51.5 x 42.5 cm,
USA

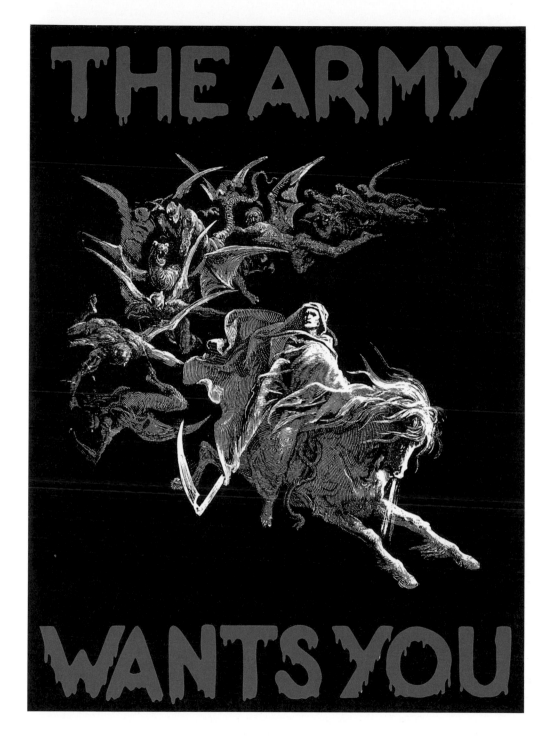

NN c. 1970. 64.5 x 46 cm, USA

446

Noordanus, George (The Netherlands 1944-)
1971. 64 x 45 cm, The Netherlands (for the election
campaign of the Pacifist Socialist Party with the
slogan 'the minority that speaks out')

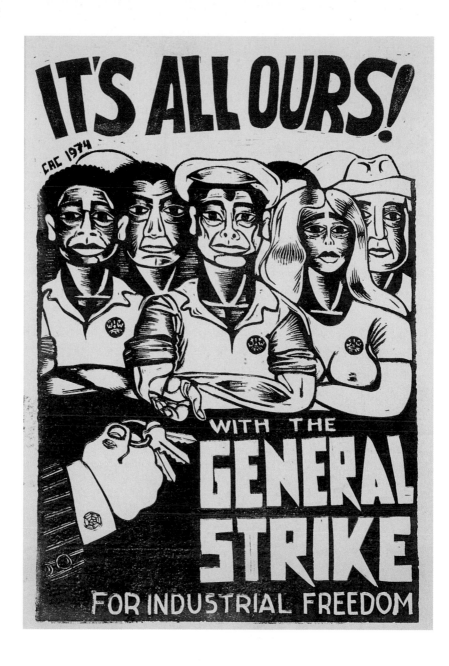

CAC 1974. 64 x 44.5 cm, United Kingdom

448

MUSÉE DES BEAUX-ARTS

PEINTRES AMÉRICAINS
CONTEMPORAINS

LILLE. 22 SEPTEMBRE
14 OCTOBRE

* LES PRESSES ARTISTIQUES · PARIS *

450

NN 1975. 62 x 38.5 cm, France

La Napoule Art Foundation   Henry Clews Memorial

10 peintres américains d'aujourd'hui

23 juin – 31 juillet

NN 60 x 42.5 cm, France

Yokoo, Tadanori (Japan 1936-) 1979. One World
Poetry. 95 x 63.5 cm, The Netherlands

P79
ONE WORLD POETRY
AMSTERDAM

DEDICATED TO JACK KEROUAC

VAN 6 T/M 14 OKTOBER 1979
OPENING 6 OKT. PARADISO-AMSTERDAM
8 T/M 14 OKT. MELKWEG-AMSTERDAM
8 T/M 14 OKT. T HOOGT-UTRECHT
Verder: Workshops/Theater/Film/Video/Dia's/Muziek
Inlichtingen: Bookingen P.O.box 14527 1013 KD Amsterdam

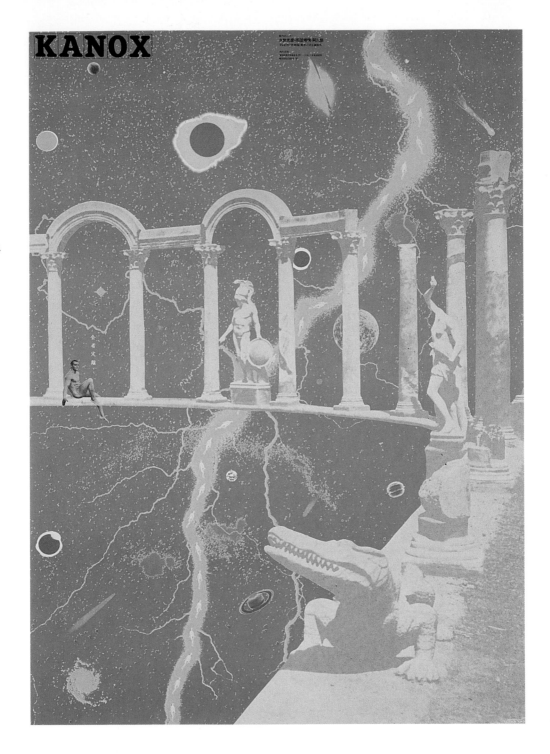

454

Yokoo, Tadanori (Japan 1936-) c. 1979. 105.5 x 73 cm, Japan

GRAPHIC

DESIGN

20TH

CENTURY

By the 1980s, instanta-
neous communications
and computer technology
radically changed the
graphic design landscape,
giving designers almost
total command of
design and production
procedures.

MEI 1986

DONDERDAG 8 MEI • KLEG • CAMBERWELL NOW • LAST POETS • HOLY TOY
VRIJDAG 9 MEI • MICHAEL NYMAN • RICHARD JOBSON • THE KLINIK • SHRUBS

Tegentonen

ZATERDAG 10 MEI • MOTOBS • THE DEADPAN TRACTOR • BUTTHOLE SURFERS • GORE
ZONDAG 11 MEI • YOUNG GODS • DAVE HOWARD SINGERS • PETER HOPE • SONIC YOUTH

PARADISO AMSTERDAM

VOORVERKOOP VANAF 25 APRIL • AUB-TICKETSHOP • NWE MUZIEKHANDEL • GET RECORDS • PLAATWERK • BOUDISQUE • RAF • ALLE AVONDEN F 10,– & LIDMAATSCHAP

ONTWERP: 1986 MAX KISMAN, GRAFISCHE VORMGEVER GEASSOCIEERDE AMSTERDAM / ABRI ABVV, AMSTERDAM

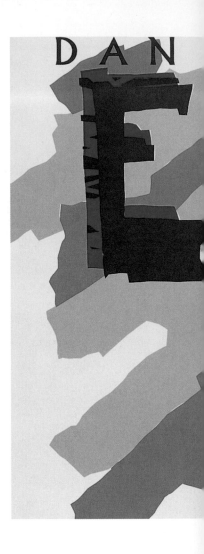

Gerard Hadders, Hard Werken (The Netherlands, Rotterdam 1954-) 1981. Poster for a dance production 'Even', Kunst Stichting, Rotterdam, The Netherlands

Caecilia roman

abcdefghijklmnop

qrstuvwxyz

1234567890

ABCDEFGHIJKLMN

OPQRSTUVWXYZ

.,-:;!?''-(*[—&%

Peter Noordzij 1961 The Netherlands. Typographer, type designer, teacher.

Fonts PMN Caecilia (1991)

PMN Caecilia Caecilia font is the premiere work of the Dutch designer Peter Matthias Noordzij. Noordzij made the first sketches of this slab serif font in 1983 during his third year of study in The Hague. Caecilia font distinguishes itself in the completeness of each of its cuts. Each comes complete with small caps and old-style figures. Such details give designers finer control over their own creations. PMN Caecilia is a trademark of Heidelberger Druckmaschinen AG, which may be registered in certain jurisdictions, exclusively licensed through Linotype Library GmbH, a wholly owned subsidiary of Heidelberger Druckmaschinen AG.

462

{ {{{ }*

EMIGRE

THE
MAGAZINE
THAT
IGNORES
BOUNDARIES

PRICE:
$7.95

Design Department

Cranbrook

graphic

design

special

Change

ISSUE

Dutch

Several Designers

Suokko, Glenn A. and Emigre Graphics Magazine
Emigre, 1988, cover

Vanderlans, Rudy and Licko, Zuzana Magazine
Emigre, 1988, page 2/3 and 32/inside back cover

This exchange between Cranbrook designers and Dutch designers manifests itself
here in a variety of forms, attitudes and
philosophies. The exchange becomes a
comparison as it exists here in print, docu-
menting time, place, the individual and
cultural identity.

We would like to thank all of the participants: Esther Vermeer, Helene Bergmans
and Valerie van Baar of Studio Dumbar, Rick Vermeulen and Laura Genninger of
Hard Werken, Harry Ahrens of Proze, Rene Delhaan of Anciënne, Lisa Anderson,
Andrew Blauvelt, Arch Garland, Allen Hori, Darrice Rossel, Susan Lally, Tamar
Rosenthal, Scott Santoro, and Scott Zukowski of Cranbrook Academy of Art Design
Department; Vincent van Baar, Eric van Casteren, Bart de Groot, Gerard van
Leyden, Max Kisman, Toni Muskie, Ron van Roon, and Holtet van der Sander
from Tel Neisenians and Edward Fella, Jeffery Keedy, Ed MacDonald, William
Samorro, Lucille Tenazas and Rudy Van der Lans from the United States for their
responses to the post cards; and Jan Jacraart and Ed MacDonald, Cranbrook
Academy of Art graduates who participated in internships in The Netherlands; Kath-
erine McCoy, CoChairman, Cranbrook Academy or Art Design Department, for her
guidance and support, and a special thank you to Roy Van der Lans for his
interest and confidence in our work and for allowing us the opportunity to
develop this issue of Emigre.

This issue

of Emigre Magazine is devoted to the exchange and transfer of culture
expressed visually and verbally by Cranbrook Academy of Art design students and
several Dutch designers. The project began when Emigre publisher, Rudy Van
der Lans, asked us to conceptualize and design an issue of Emigre Magazine
focusing our attention on graphic design and the exchange between the
Cranbrook Academy of Art Design Department and several Dutch design groups
including Studio Dumbar, Den Haag, and Hard Werken, Rotterdam. Individual
Dutch designers from Proze, Cranbrook Industrial Design, Eindhoven, Toni Dimor,
Amsterdam and Voor Vije, Amsterdam, also contributed to the project. The
following are individual proposals and design solutions which all deal with
cultural and cross-cultural stereotypes, experiences, and expectations. Each
Cranbrook Design student proposed a design problem to individual Dutch
designers. The proposals were devoted toward individual interpretation and/
or expression of the designer's particular culture. Cranbrook Design students
responded to their own proposals as well. The ongoing exchange that takes place between Cranbrook design students,
Dutch design studios and Dutch visiting artists has been an enriching and inspir-
ing experience for everyone involved. Among Dutch visiting artists to Cranbrook
are Gert Dumbar, Studio Dumbar; Rick Vermeulen, Hard Werken; Professor R. D. Oostraat
of the PTT, and Anton Beeke. Design students from Cranbrook Academy of Art
participate yearly in internships with Studio Dumbar and most recently with Proze,
Toni Dimor and Voor Vije. The exchange exceeds beyond graphic design, as many
lasting friendships and professional relationships have developed over the
years. More importantly, it has been the cultural exchange that has had the most
profound effect on each individual. In understanding culture we must compare
cultures. In describing our own cultures, we learn about other cultures. In
discussing the differences or similarities between cultures, we define our own
culture.

culture THE NETHERLANDS

several Dutch designers

TRAN

CODE BLEU

CODE BLEU

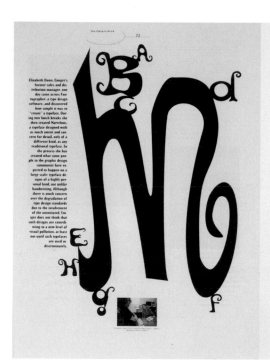

Elizabeth Dunn, Emigre's former sales and distribution manager, one day came across Fontographer, a type design software, and discovered how simple it was to "create" a typeface. During two lunch breaks she then created Marvelous, a typeface designed with as much intent and concern for detail, only of a different kind, as any traditional typeface. In the process she has created what some people in the graphic design community have expected to happen on a large scale: typeface designs of a highly personal kind, not unlike handwriting. Although there is much concern over the degradation of type design standards due to the involvement of the uninitiated, Emigre does not think that such designs are contributing to a new level of visual pollution, at least not until such typefaces are used in discriminately.

Design Nirvana
by: John Weber

why (y) something (s) is (is).

Hmmm.

3...days atCran-Brook

EMIGRE Nº19: Starting From Zero

Ó

In this issue Emigre asks the question "Does all experimentation in graphic design eventually lead to the simplification of graphic design?" In true modernist fashion, albeit loosely interpreted, the entire issue is set in one typeface, a sans serif (Template Gothic designed by Barry Deck), and all texts are set flush left, ragged right.

INTRRR ODUCT ION

COVERS

Emigre No. 22. Price

ck Bell Ni

Culprits

RAMATIZATIO

COVERS

neo-mania Nº 24

Anthon Beeke (The Netherlands, Amsterdam 1940-)
1990, The Netherlands

abcdefghijklmno

pqrstuvwxyz

1234567890

ABCDEFGHIJKLMN

OPQRSTUVWXYZ

.,-:;!?"'-(*[—&%

Erik van Blokland 1967 The Netherlands. Dutch type designer. He founded the **LettError** virtual type foundry together with Just van Rossum. They also worked together at **MetaDesign**. Fame came with the release of **Beowolf** (co-designed with van Rossum), a font whose ragged edges shift randomly each time the font is printed. Another font of his, **Kosmik**, has a version that flips between three alternates for each character for a more friendly, hand-drawn feel. He is a key developer on the Robofog project with **Just van Rossum** and **Peter van Blokland**. The flipper technique is designed by Van Rossum.

Kosmik RandomFonts are a blunt way to create liveliness in the text. A FlipperFont contains a number of alternative letters that will be called for in the right order. Kosmik is the first LettError FlipperFont intended for public use. It contains three alternatives for each letter. During printing each letter is followed by a letter from the next alternative: one-two-three-one-... If there are three identical letters on a row, they will thus be given different outlines. The fourth and first letter are from the same font, but by then they are so far apart that a possible sameness in the contours does not matter as much.

There are other ways in which a FlipperFont can function. For instance, it can switch between two fonts regularly and only use the third font once in a random number (30) of characters. The way in which the FlipperFont is programmed has effect on the texture the typeface makes on the page; it is an integral part of its design.

FF Kosmik OT
Autofflippperr*
0123456789012345678 9
Plain & **Bold** ¶ ✈ ⊕
✱In OpenType Savvy Applications
Liveliness, Onomatopaea
MACOS+WIN, SCREEN+PRINT
OpenTypeFontFont

Index

Colophon

Design
Cees W. de Jong, Jan Johan ter Poorten,
V+K Publishing/Design, Laren

Photography
Arthur Martin, Bussum

Lithography
Fritz Repro, Almere

Printing
Snoeck-Ducaju & Zoon, Ghent

With special thanks to Linotype Library GmbH,
Otmar Hoefer for kindly supplying the following
Linotype fonts: Apollo, Caecilia, Electra,
Franklin Gothic, Optima, Sabon and Univers
and to Henk W.J. Gianotten for advice and assistance
regarding the fonts.

Martijn F. Le Coultre
By trade a notary, Le Coultre is an avid collector of
modernist books and posters and is an expert on
their history. He lives in Laren, The Netherlands.

Alston W. Purvis
Is director of the Visual Arts Division of the School
for the Arts at Boston University and is the author of
'Dutch Graphic Design, 1918-1945'.

Both cooperated on various publications, including
'Wendingen, 1918-1932' and 'A Century of Posters'.

Cees W. de Jong
Designer and publisher, born in 1945 in Amsterdam,
The Netherlands. In 1970 he graduated from the
Gerrit Rietveld Academy and since 1975 has been
director of V+K Publishing/Design, which specializes
in publishing and designing international co-editions
on architecture and design.

Jan Johan ter Poorten
Graphic designer, born in 1964 in Vlissingen,
The Netherlands. After graduating from the Royal
Academy for Art and Design, 's-Hertogenbosch, in
1988, he gained practical experience working for a
Dutch publisher and two UK design studios.

Since 1989 both have been working together at
V+K Publishing/Design on numerous international
book projects in the fields of design, art, and architecture for a wide range of co-publishers throughout
the world.